To Lisa
From Grandmother

Christmas, '78'

To Lisa
From Grandmother

Bible Stories

as told by

Norman Vincent Peale

Illustrations by

Grabianski

Banner Press, Inc.
New York
1978

To my children
and grandchildren,
to whom I have told
these wonderful Bible stories

Library of Cóngress Cataloging in Publication Data

Peale, Norman Vincent, 1898—
Bible stories.

2. Bible stories, English. I. Title.
BS5 50.2P4   220.9'505   73-4481
ISBN 0-531-02634-5

Introduction: What the Bible Says to Us Today

Why did I decide to write a book of Bible stories when so many splendid volumes on the same subject have already been written? Certainly it was not because I might produce a book that would be superior to others. It was only that I have certain convictions about the Bible that I felt should be shared with readers and especially with young people.

Of course the Bible is filled with some of the most interesting, even thrilling, stories ever told. And since there is endless variety and meaning in the stories, they bear telling and retelling by anyone who, loving the greatest of all books, believes that a new and fresh emphasis upon its relevance to the modern world can be helpful.

My particular viewpoint is that the Bible is the most contemporary and timeless book ever written. It is as new as tomorrow morning's newspaper and in greater depth. It applies today no less than in former times, indeed perhaps more importantly than ever, considering the overwhelming spiritual needs of our generation.

The Bible relates specifically and directly to every problem of individuals and society at large. For this reason I have endeavored to retell these Biblical stories not only in modern language forms but also with a view toward modern thought concepts.

Hopefully the reader, especially the young reader, will come to realize that the Bible is more—much more—than a musty and dusty old-time book written generations ago. His mind and imagination will be challenged by fact that in the Bible narratives are to be found workable answers to his every question. He will find creative solutions to all of his problems. He will see that truly this is the book of life...notably his life. The Bible shows the young person how to have the best that he wants from life.

My earnest desire in retelling these Bible stories is to make the greatest book ever written come alive as the handbook, the rule book, the guidebook for living now in the now generation.

Norman Vincent Peale

Contents

The Old Testament

Out of Nothingness

In the beginning God . . .

With these four majestic words begins the greatest book ever written. Everything that surrounds us, from the tiniest speck of invisible matter to the greatest galaxy in outer space, had to start somewhere. The Bible begins by telling us that there was— and is—only one Source of everything, the infinite Source that we groping human beings call God.

The Story of Creation is intended to be awe-inspiring—and it is. Instantly, without apology or preamble, it forces us to think about ideas that are too big for our limited minds. "And the earth was without form," says the second verse of Genesis, the first book of the Bible, "and void." How can we visualize complete nothingness? We can't, any more than we can grasp the concept of infinite space, or infinite time. But then, in the same verse, the Bible tells us that the Spirit of God moved . . . and when it moved, out of nothingness came everything.

What did God do first? He spoke four words: "Let there be light." Try to imagine, if you can, what it was like when the first radiance burst upon the blackness that was not just the absence of light but the absence of everything. What a stupendous moment! What an awesome burst of purposeful power! Some modern astronomers believe that the universe began with just such an inconceivable explosion that flung the nebulae like fiery pinwheels into outer space

where they are receding still. Maybe so. The Bible tells us that however it happened, the original decision was made in the mind of God.

That this first manifestation of that Spirit was light is not surprising. Light is the source of all life. Without it, nothing lives, nothing grows. Without it there can be no warmth, no seedtime, no harvest. From the beginning, God knew all this. The Bible tells us that He ended the first incredible day of creation by dividing light from darkness, calling one Day and the other Night.

This first mind-stretching chapter of Genesis goes on to describe how the whole of Creation was carried out in just six days. Some people believe that each of those days consisted literally of twenty-four hours. Others think that each day is a symbolic way of describing the passage of millions of years. I feel sure, myself, that God could have done what the Bible says He did in six days, or in six hours, or in six seconds, if it had suited Him. The work of Creation is above and beyond mere time.

That first day saw the creation of light, and its division from darkness.

On the second day God made the firmament, or the vault of the sky.

On the third day He created the land and the seas, and He ordered the earth to bring forth grass and plants and trees.

On the fourth day He made "two great lights," one to rule the day and the other to rule the night. It is interesting that the author of Genesis did not name the two heavenly bodies, perhaps because they were objects of worship among more primitive peoples. In any case, on the fourth day the sun and moon came into being. And the Bible adds, in words of staggering simplicity, "the stars also." Think of it! Millions of solar systems. Billions of stars. "He made the stars also."

On the fifth day life appeared. "And God said, Let the waters bring forth abundantly the moving creature that hath life, and fowl that may fly above the earth...." How astounding is the way these ancient writings anticipate the scientists of today, who tell us that life did begin in the prehistoric seas. Imagine those silent oceans suddenly filled with the endless variety of fishes and sea animals that persist to this day—"great whales," the Bible says, but also the rainbow colors of the dolphin, the leaping salmon, the lordly tarpon, the tiny flying fish skittering their silver tracks across the furrows of the deep. Imagine, too, how different it was when the cawing of crows and the music of songbirds first rose above the meadows and the treetops. No wonder God "saw that it was good."

On the sixth day God created the living creatures of the earth, each one capable of reproducing its own kind. Note how in the Genesis story living creatures appear in ascending order of complexity. This, too, was part of God's plan, because on this sixth and final day, at the very end of the stupendous process of Creation, God decided to bring into existence the most complex creature of all, a creature fashioned in His own image, the creature known as man.

The second chapter of Genesis tells us vividly how God did it. He took the dust of the earth. Carefully, gently, like a master potter shaping an exquisite vase, He formed a noble figure, clean-limbed, symmetrical, but still lifeless. Then, the Bible says, the Lord God "breathed into his nostrils the breath of life; and man became a living soul."

What a magnificent concept it is: the spirit of God impinging upon a handful of dust and bringing it to life! And what a thought for each of us to keep in mind, the thought that without the spirit of God permeating us, we are not really alive at all, but just inanimate clay.

Not only did God create man, He created a place for man to live, a garden "eastward in Eden." That name "Eden" comes from an ancient word meaning "fertile plain." And this garden was fertile indeed. In it grew "every tree that is pleasant to the sight, and good for food." Weeds and briars were unknown. There was a crystal river to drink from. The days were warm and golden, the nights gentle and scented with the perfume of flowers and the smell of ripening fruit. In this paradise even the animals lived together in peace and harmony. The Bible says that the Lord brought them all to Adam, to see what he would call them, and Adam gave a name "to all cattle, and to the fowl of the air, and to every beast of the field."

But each of these creatures had a mate, and Adam had none. Was he unhappy about this? The Bible does not say. Perhaps he was, because he could observe that he alone had no counterpart. In any case, it was the Lord Who decided that "it is not good that the man should be alone," and so He caused a deep sleep to fall upon Adam. While the man slept, God took one of his ribs and from it fashioned a woman. Then He woke Adam from his sleep and brought the woman to him.

Observe the symbolism of this remarkable story. In the case of all other living things, male and female were created separately. Only in the case of man was his mate formed out of a part of himself, a part very close to his heart. This meant that a man and wife could never be totally separate and distinct individuals; they would always be one flesh. As Adam himself put it, speaking of this lovely creature that had been presented to him, "This is now bone of my bones, and flesh of my flesh: she shall be called Woman because she was taken out of Man."

So Adam and his new companion, Eve, began an existence in which there were none of the thorns of life as we know it. No guilt. No shame. No disappointment. No disease. No fear of death, for there was no death. Perhaps there was some work—after all, the Lord had put Adam in charge of the garden "to dress it and to keep it." But the work must have been light and pleasant, just enough to keep him occupied and to give him a sense of achievement. The man and the woman must have watched the days slide by like beads on a goden chain, confident that they would never end.

And perhaps they never would have ended, except for one thing. In creating man as a rational being, God had granted him free will. Man could do as he pleased. He had a choice. If he had had no free will, no choice, he would have been a soulless automaton, no better than the animals. But because the Lord had breathed upon him, he had a soul, and because he had a soul he also had the power of choice—and the woman had it too.

Now there were, in the middle of the garden of Eden, two mighty trees. Both bore marvelous fruits. One was the tree of the knowledge of good and evil. The other was the tree of life. God had given Adam permission to eat the fruit of every other tree in the garden, but He had specifically forbidden him to touch or taste the fruit of the tree of knowledge of good and evil. "For in the day that thou eatest thereof," said the Lord to Adam, "thou shalt surely die."

The punishment attached to this order showed how important it was. It was so important that this commandment was given to Adam before Eve was created, while

he was still alone. And yet, while God could give such an order, He could not force either Adam or Eve to obey. This was a limitation that He had placed upon Himself. They could use their free will to obey or disobey Him.

Left to themselves, I like to think that Adam and Eve would have remained obedient. Why not? God had created them out of a handful of dust. He had designed and brought into being a paradise for them ot live in. He had given them dominion over all other creatures in it. In return for this extraordinary kindness, what did He ask? Obedience in one thing. Surely this was not asking much! If there was an ounce of gratitude in Adam's heart—and there must have been—he would not have felt at all inclined to displease such a kind Creator. The idea of disobedience would have had to come

from the outside. It did—and it came from a source against which Adam, being a man, had little defense. It came from a new force that somehow had invaded the garden. It came in the form of a serpent, but inside the serpent was the Spirit of Rebellion Against God.

How did the new spirit get into the

garden? The Bible does not say. The presence of evil in the world was a mystery then, just as it is a mystery now. But that there is such a force, acting through man's capacity for free will, none of us can deny.

"Now," says the Bible, "the serpent was more subtle than any beast of the field which the Lord God had made." Subtle, yes; cunning, yes; but also much more than that. He must have had a tremendous personality, enormous powers of persuasion, to seduce and confuse Eve the way he did. I wonder, sometimes, what he looked like when he first approached the woman. I doubt if he looked like an ordinary snake, as he is sometimes drawn, slyly coiled around the trunk of a tree. I think he must have been a magnificent creature, tall and erect, dressed in brilliant colors. Perhaps, if he was Lucifer himself, the fallen archangel that tradition says he was, he came upon the wife of Adam in all the somber splendor of the Prince of Darkness.

In any case, he made her obedience to the commandment of God seem like stupidity or cowardice or both. He told her that the punishment God had warned of would not happen. He made it sound as if God were afraid that His own creation—man—might rival Him. He made it seem as if the advantages to be gained from ignoring God's orders would outweigh the disadvantages. Eve was no match for him. "She took of the fruit thereof, and did eat." Then, knowing that what she had done was wrong, but wanting companionship in her wrongdoing (nothing is lonelier than solitary guilt), she took some of the fruit to Adam. No doubt she used the same arguments on her husband that the serpent had used on her. Perhaps he hesitated. But in the end, partly because he loved his wife, partly because some little arrogant spark in him wanted the forbidden knowledge, he let himself be persuaded... "and he did eat."

Instantly everything was changed. The Bible says that their eyes were opened, and they knew that they were naked. They sewed fig leaves together and made themselves aprons. But the guilt in their minds went deeper than that. What they really wanted was a shield or a screen from the sin of using their God-given free will to defy God. For this they knew that the fig leaves were not enough, and so they "hid themselves from the presence of the Lord God amongst the trees of the garden."

But every wrongdoer knows it is not easy to hid from God. In fact, it is impossible. So soon the guilty pair heard the Lord calling them. When He asked Adam if he had disobeyed Him, Adam—all too human— hastily tried to pin the blame on his wife. When the Lord asked Eve what she had done, she was equally quick to blame the serpent.

Since all three shared the guilt, God decreed that each should be punished. The proud serpent henceforth would crawl in the dust and be feared and hated by mankind. The woman would bear children in pain and, instead of being equal to her husband as she had been, would be subservient to him. As for Adam, the generous earth would no longer support him with no effort on his part. He would have to struggle to stay alive, paying for existence with the sweat of his brow. Limits, too, were set upon his life; he could no longer count on happy days forever. He and his wife and all their descendants would have to return, ultimately, to the dust from whence they had come. So the wages of sin, the sin of disobedience, were death, as God had warned them. And each descendant of Adam has to pay that penalty still.

Nor did the Lord allow the man and his wife to remain in the peaceful garden that had been created for their enjoyment. They still had the gift of free will. God knew that at any time they might use it to disobey Him again. They might even try to gain immortality by tasting the fruit of the other forbidden tree, the tree of life itself. So He drove them out of the garden and placed a guard of cherubim, and a flaming sword, to make sure that they did not return.

Even then, though, His kindness and concern for the two sinners remained. The Bible says that He made coats of skins for these erring children of His, and clothed him. Implicit in this gesture, I think, is the promise that God did not intend to let man

stay alienated from Him forever.

In the first three chapters, then, of this amazing book you can find answers to the deepest questions that haunt mankind, questions about the meaning of the universe, of life, of sin, of evil, of pain and suffering and death. If you were to read just these three chapters every day for a month—and I would earnestly urge you to do just that—you would not even begin to reach all the depths or unlock all the treasure chests that it contains.

But you might—indeed you would—begin to understand why this Book of Books overshadows all others that have ever been written, "towering aloft into the blue secrets of Heaven."

This mighty panorama, this epic of God and man and destiny, was meant for all men in all nations at all times. Let us go forward and explore it together.

The First Homicide

One wonders sometimes what it was like for Adam and Eve the first night after they were driven out of Paradise. It must have been pretty miserable. Perhaps they were hungry. Perhaps they were cold. Perhaps they were afraid of wild beasts that certainly were no longer the friendly animals of the Garden of Eden. And if they were miserable physically, what about their state of mind? They knew that they had offended God. They knew, for the first time, the pangs of guilt. They knew, too, that they could no longer live indefinitely. Now they were mortal. The word itself means doomed to death.

So it must have been a deeply unhappy pair of humans who crouched in some cave or took refuge in some tall tree and waited for the warming rays of the sun. Did Adam blame Eve for their predicament? The Bible offers us no clue. Perhaps he did, but I like to believe that in this fallen man were still some sparks of divinity. After all, he was still made in the image of God. I like to think that there was courage in him, and determination to make a new start, and the hope that somehow, eventually, he would regain the favor of the Creator.

In any case, the man and the woman faced up to their new life bravely. Adam began tilling the soil; Eve became a mother, first of a boy named Cain, then of a second son named Abel.

From the start, apparently, these two sons of Adam were very different. Abel was a keeper of sheep, which meant that he was a nomad, moving from place to place in search of grazing land. Cain was a farmer, a "tiller of the ground," which meant that he stayed in one place. There has always been a clash of personalities between the restless rover and the stolid stay-at-home. Also, since the world began there has been some rivalry, some jealousy, some friction between the children in any family.

Adam and Even must have taught their sons to love the Lord, because we first see them trying to please Him. Cain brought an offering of the crops that he had grown. Abel offered lambs from his flocks. Perhaps these offerings were made in an effort to win God's favor; perhaps they were simply in gratitude for the gift of life. In any case, we are told that Abel's offering found favor in the sight of the Lord, and Cain's did not.

Why was Cain's offering less pleasing? We don't know. Perhaps his motives in making the offering were less worthy than Abel's. Perhaps he was already harboring a grudge against his younger brother because he thought his mother favored him, or his father preferred him.... That sort of thing, too, has been going on since the world began. In any case, the Lord made it clear that He preferred Abel's offering. Full of resentment, Cain brooded about it until one day his self-control gave way. He "talked with Abel," which probably means that there was a fierce argument. Full of fury, Cain "rose up against Abel his brother, and slew him."

Did he actually mean to kill him? Again, we don't know. Cain knew what death was, all right; he had seen animals die. But no human being had ever died at the hand of another human being. Indeed, no human

25

being had ever died at all. We can imagine Cain staring down at the lifeless form with growing horror and self-condemnation. We can imagine, too, his panic when he heard the Lord asking where Abel was.

"I don't know," Cain replied, and he added a question that has haunted mankind ever since: "Am I my brother's keeper?"

The Lord did not answer that question directly, but He made it clear that Cain had committed a grievous crime. The penalty was banishment, a terrible punishment indeed to the stay-at-home Cain who preferred to live securely in one place, tending his crops. Cain cried out that he could not bear it, adding that wherever he went strangers would try to kill him. The Lord replied that He would protect Cain's life by setting a mark upon him, so that strangers would know who he was and would not harm him. The Bible doesn't say what that mark was; perhaps it was some form of tattoo that desert tribesmen used far back in the dawn of history. In any case, grievous though Cain's crime was, the Lord allowed him to live and find a wife and have a son named Enoch and even build a city that he named after his son.

What does the story of Cain and Abel have to say to us today? In one way it is a warning that, even though we are all children of Adam and therefore are made in God's image, we also have buried deep within us the savagery and fury that will lead us to murder unless we learn to control and subdue such impulses. After all, what is war in the twentieth century except the crime of Cain magnified a thousand times and given official sanction? All the human beings on this earth are brothers and sisters under the fatherhood of God. Someday, God willing, the human family will learn to live as a family should.

The other message of the story of Cain and Abel is a more encouraging one. It is that even though a person makes a terrible mistake, that does not mean his life is over. Cain was a murderer, and yet he went on to establish a city. He made his mistake, he took his just punishment, he kept going, and in the end he was able to do something constructive and good.

God promises to forgive us our sins if we are sorry for them and resolve not to repeat them. Forgiveness, then, is nothing but a chance to do better. God gave Cain that chance, and he took it. So can we.

The Fantastic Voyage

In the early days of the world, according to the Bible, men lived to almost incredible ages. Perhaps their diets were more nutritious than ours are today. Perhaps they had fewer emotional strains and stresses to endure. Perhaps they were given longer life in order to populate the vast empty spaces around them. In any case, we're told that they lived for hundreds of years.

Adam himself, the first man, was nine hundred and thirty years old when he died. Adam's third son, Seth, lived to be nine hundred and twelve. If you assume that under normal circumstances three generations will appear every century, these men were able to look upon twenty-five or thirty generations of descendants before they died.

The record for old age, as everyone knows, is held by Methuselah. He lived for nine hundred and sixty-nine years. Just what he accomplished, if anything, we don't know. Perhaps if you live that long, accomplishments don't matter!

But despite all this long life, God was not pleased with the way things were going on the earth he had created. As time went by, people grew corrupt and "the earth was filled with violence." In his anger, God said, "I will destory man whom I have created from the face of the earth; both man, and beast... for it repenteth me that I have made them."

Fortunately for all of us, God decided to make an exception in the case of one good man and his family. The man was named Noah; he had three sons: Shem, Ham, and Japheth. The Lord warned Noah that the earth was going to have a devastating flood. All living creatures, except for a chosen few, would perish. The ones destined to survive would take refuge in a great ship called an ark. And Noah was ordered to build it.

If ever a man showed blind, unquestioning faith, it was Noah. He lived far inland where floods never came. He knew nothing about the sea, or about boats. The Lord even had to tell him how to make the ark watertight! Now, suddenly, he was told to start building an oceangoing vessel roughly the size of a modern tanker. But he didn't hesitate. He didn't ask questions. He just did what the Lord told him to do.

How his friends and neighbors must have stared when Noah began pacing off three hundred cubits—about four hundred and seventy-five feet—which was to be the length of the ark. How they must have laughed when he told them that a flood was coming that would drown them all. They must have agreed among themselves that the old man had become senile. No doubt it became a form of neighborhood entertainment to go out and watch as the huge vessel slowly took shape, to ridicule the old man and jeer at his strongly muscled, sunburned sons.

Perhaps among the onlookers there were a few who felt a twinge of uneasiness as the dogged old patriarch, already six hundred years old, supervised the loading of the ark with tons of provisions. What if this crazy old eccentric turned out to be right? But none, apparently, felt uneasy enough to ask to be included in the fantastic voyage. When long columns of animals began to wind down out of the hills and across the plains, then undoubtedly some of the bystanders did become alarmed, because this, surely, was no ordinary happening. But by that time it was too late either to try to join forces with Noah or to build their own means of salvation.

It must have taken several days and nights to load all the creatures aboard. The largest beasts like the elephants and hippopotamuses were probably down on the lowest level. No doubt the gentle grazing animals had to be segregated from the big cats. There must have been a bedlam of sound with hyenas laughing and donkeys braying and lions roaring and endless rows of birds on endless perches twittering and chirping. A place had to be found for "every creeping thing." Of animals particularly useful to man, Noah was ordered to take seven pair, just to make sure that when the floods were over those species would multiply rapidly.

The account of the deluge in Genesis is wonderfully specific. The rains began on the seventeenth day of the second month. Slowly at first, then with increasing violence, the downpour came. The people of those days

believed that above the vault of the sky were mighty waters, and that when the "windows of heaven" were open, the water would pour through. Now it did, falling in sheets, in torrents, drumming like thunder on the roof of the ark, pouring over the riverbanks, flooding the valleys, engulfing houses and temples, sweeping away whole cities. Men and beasts fled to higher ground, but their flight was in vain. For forty days and forty nights the downpour continued. The waters rose until even the tallest mountains were submerged and nothing was left but an

endless expanse of angry, heaving water.

Vivid as it is, this account in Genesis is not the only story of a deluge that has come down to us through the centuries. In almost every primitive culture are similar stories and legends. So uniform are some of these accounts that they all seem to point to the same mighty catastrophe back in the dawn of time.

Archaeology, too, has things to say about the Flood. Not many years ago, digging into the mound of earth that marked the site of ancient Ur, archaeologist Leonard Woolley came upon a stratum of clay more than eight feet thick. Forty feet down, it contained no shards, no rubbish, no manmade relics of any kind, although there were such relics both above and below it. To lay down such a deposit of clay, geologists said, would have required a tremendous and protracted flood in the ancient land of Sumer. Thus, once again, science seems to confirm the words of the sacred Book.

For a hundred and fifty days the ark and its cargo floated upon the empty surface of a limitless sea. Five long months of monotony and cramped quarters, of desperately hard work (all those animals had to be fed!) and uncertainty. Noah and his family must have grown discouraged at times. Had God forgotten all about them? Was the earth drowned forever? Would their provisions hold out? But "God remembered Noah." What a day it must have been for them—the seventeenth day of the seventh month— when the keel grated on something solid and

moments later the ark was aground "upon the mountains of Ararat."

For forty more days Noah waited while the waters gradually subsided. Then he let a raven go, and a dove, "to see if the waters were abated." The strong-winged raven flew to and fro, but the dove came back exhausted. Noah waited another week, then sent her out again. This time she returned with an olive leaf in her mouth, and so the weary voyagers knew that somewhere cultivated land was reppearing.

This scene of the gentle bird returning and of Noah's joy as he "put forth his hand, and took her, and pulled her in unto him into the ark" is one of the most touching and reassuring in the whole Bible. It symbolizes the resurgence of hope after a dark time of difficulty and distress. It means that while floods and dangers and uncertainties occur in every life, the man who trusts God will come through intact. It means, too, that if people will just hang on long enough in times of trouble, God will send a sign, when the testing period is almost over, that good things lie ahead for those who keep the faith and refuse to admit defeat.

In Noah's case, the olive leaf was just the forerunner of a far greater promise. After he and the animals had come safely out of the ark, and after he had offered a sacrifice of thanksgiving, God established a mighty covenant or agreement with him. Never again, God promised, would the earth be so devastated by water. The sign of the covenant was the mighty rainbow, arching from horizon to horizon in a blaze of brilliant color against the dark storm clouds. "I do set my bow in the cloud," said the Lord, and He added that His promise was good "for perpetual generations."

Noah and his sons were ordered to "be fruitful, and multiply, and replenish the earth." They took up their great task with confidence and enthusiasm, heartened by God's promise that "while the earth remaineth, seedtime and harvest, and cold and heat, and summer and winter, and day and night shall not cease."

It was a new dawn, a new day, a fresh start for all mankind.

The Tower of Pride

In the eleventh chapter of the Book of Genesis is a remarkable short short story. It's completely contained in nine verses—less than three hundred words—but it paints such vivid mental pictures that it has fascinated hearers for at least thirty centuries.

In this story, the descendants of Noah find "a plain in the land of Shinar" and decide to live there. Presumably they prosper greatly and reach a high stage of civilization. They are ambitious, energetic people who are highly unified. They all speak the same language. They all like to get things done. They have a very high opinion of themselves and finally, as a direct reflection of this high opinion, they decide to build a city and a tower so high that it will reach all the way up to Heaven.

They are skilled brickmakers, so they set to work with thousands of laborers and millions of bricks to make this presumptuous dream come true. And they are well on their way to succeeding when God intervenes. He doesn't like the arrogance of these people who consider themselves better than anyone else. He decides to take them down a peg or two.

How did He do it? He "did there confound the language of all the earth" so that the builders of the great tower, the Tower of Babel, could no longer understand one another. Imagine that scene: the astonishment, the dismay, the confusion, the angry shouting. No one able to transmit or obey an order. No one able to explain or carry out a plan. In the face of this total frustration, all work ceased. The great tower stood unfinished, looming against the sky. And gradually it fell into decay, because the workers split into countless groups, each with its own language, and the Lord "did scatter them abroad upon the face of all the earth."

Undoubtedly one purpose of this story of the Tower of Babel was to explain to ancient peoples how all the languages and dialects of the earth came into being. Beyond that, the tower itself may be a historical echo—and criticism—of the soaring pagan temples of Ur or even the pyramids of Egypt, constructed with so much effort and human suffering to so little purpose. But the deeper message, surely, is that confusion awaits those who, in their blind pride, think that they can "get to the top" solely by their own efforts, who assume that they can do whatever they please without the help or approval of God.

If the Tower of Babel does stand for man's pride in his own accomplishments, that lesson seems even more pertinent today. Our amazing technology has let us defeat most diseases, probe into the heart of the atom, put human beings on the moon... achievements so tremendous that arrogance is their almost inevitable sequel. If a man can do such godlike things, the Devil whispers, what need does he have of God?

The answer—and perhaps this is what the story of Babel is trying to tell us—is that the more advanced our technology becomes, the more we need God. The more complex our culture, the greater grows the danger of alienation, not only from God, but from one another. In this astounding century of ours, we speak increasingly of gaps: a generation gap, a communication gap, a knowledge gap, an education gap. Already the language of science has become so complex that specialists in one field have difficulty understanding specialists in another. As our tower of civilization grows higher, so does our difficulty in understanding one another.

What we need today is what the builders of Babel lacked—a willingness to admit our own limitations and shortcomings, a willingness to curb the sin of pride, a willingness to listen for the voice of God.

The message of the Tower of Babel is clear and simple: put God first. If a nation does this, it will complete its greatest projects and realize its proudest dreams. If it doesn't, in the end confusion will come upon it, and its people will be "scattered abroad on the face of the whole earth."

The Man Who Was God's Friend

Almost four thousand years ago, in the sun-baked land known today as Iraq, a remarkable child was born. Three great religions claim him as a spiritual ancestor. To the early Hebrews, he was known as Abram; to later Jews and to Christians as Abraham; to Muslims as Ibrahim. To all of them he was "the friend of God," one of the first men in the dawn of history to realize that behind the jumble of bloodthirsty pagan gods was a single Supreme Being, Creator of everything, and constantly mindful of His creature, man.

The Bible tells us that Terah, Abram's father, settled in the ancient city of Ur on the banks of the muddy Euphrates River, and it was there that Abram grew to manhood. At the time, two separate races were living peaceably together in Ur: the Semites, from whom Terah and his family were descended, and the Sumerians, a gifted, dark-haired people who had settled in Mesopotamia (the "land between the rivers") a thousand years earlier, bringing with them wheeled vehicles and a knowledge of mathematics and one of the earliest forms of writing. Under the Sumerians, the city of Ur had risen to great heights, with craftsmen in jewels and precious metals whose skill has never been surpassed. But by the time Abram was born, those proud and prosperous days were over, and Ur was beginning to fall into stagnation and decay.

Suppose we were able to look back from this age of television and spaceships to the Ur of four thousand years ago—what would Abram's boyhood have been like? In some ways, not too different from the life of a boy today. Since his father was a man of importance, he undoubtedly went to school. He would have learned to read and write, not letters as we know them, but wedge-shaped marks on tablets of wet clay that hardened into almost indestructible bricks. Archaeologists have found thousands of such tablets, some of them clearly the "homework" of schoolchildren. Abram would have studied arithmetic: some of the tablets show problems in square root. He would not have had to struggle with decimals because the ancient Sumerians were more likely to divide things into sixths than into tenths. The twelve hours on our clocks, our custom of counting eggs by the dozen, the three hundred and sixty degrees in a circle—these things come down to us from the Sumerians.

Abram would have studied astronomy, too. He would have been familiar with hundreds of pagan gods, particularly the moon god who was the patron deity of Ur and whose temple was on top of a huge tower of terraced brick known as a *ziggurat*—the word means "heaven," or "the-place-where-the-god-dwells." On certain days the young boy would have watched priests bringing the moon-god idol down the long flights of steps to the music of harps and cymbals. He would have seen the citizens of Ur offering doves or lambs to the priests as sacrifices and receiving in return receipts printed quickly and clearly on a clay tablet with a wedge-shaped stick.

The city was dusty and shabby in many areas, but it was a colorful place. There were no horses or camels, but there were chariots and wagons drawn by long-eared donkeys, and sailing ships that brought cargoes up from the Persian Gulf. Houses were made of brick, often two-storeyed, with blank walls on the street to keep out dust and noise and a pleasant courtyard inside surrounded by balconies. In the marketplace businessmen haggled and complained about hard times, sighing that things were better "in the old days." They were saying it four thousand years ago, and they are saying it still.

An ancient legend says that Abram's father, Terah, was a maker of idols, and that as a boy Abram sold these images of clay in the streets of Ur. The legend, which is recorded in the Jewish *Book of Jubilees*, written three centuries before Christ, relates that Abram finally reproached his father for such idolatry. "What can these statues do for anyone?" he is supposed to have said. "They are nothing but bits of clay. The true God cannot dwell in such lifeless things!"

Only a legend, but sometimes legend is a shimmering cloak for truth. In any case, we know from the Bible that the time did come when Terah decided to leave Ur. The reason is not given. Perhaps it was economic: bad times, declining business. Perhaps it was dissatisfaction with the paganism that surrounded him. Anyway, Terah left, taking with him his son Abram, and Abram's wife, Sarai, and a grandson whose name was Lot. They settled in the town of Haran, and there Terah finally died. This left Abram the leader of the clan, with his nephew, Lot, as second-in-command.

Now God had been watching Abram, and what He saw must have pleased Him, because one day when Abram was in his seventy-sixth year the Lord spoke to him suddenly, giving him an order and making him a promise. The order was simply to leave Haran and "get thee . . . unto a land that I will show thee." The promise was magnificently unconditional: "I will make of thee a great nation . . . in thee shall all families of the earth be blessed." One might almost say that the remainder of this extraordinary collection of writings that we call the Bible is the story of how that great promise to Abram was fulfilled—and is still being fulfilled.

So Abram and Lot assembled their caravans. Driving their sheep and cattle before them, they moved slowly south into the land of Canaan at the eastern end of the Mediterranean Sea, the territory of modern Israel. There a famine made them push on eventually into Egypt, but when the famine was over they came back. By now the herds of Abram and Lot were so great that there was not enough grazing land for all the animals. Their herdsmen were beginning to quarrel, and so the two leaders agreed to separate peacefully. Abram remained in Canaan, on a plain belonging to a man called Mamre. Lot went to live in the city of Sodom near the shores of the Dead Sea.

The valley of the Jordan river was a pleasant place, but it was constantly being fought over by petty kings and tribal chieftains. At one point Lot and his family were made prisoners and carried away by some of these marauders. When he heard of it, the peaceful Abram armed some of his own followers, pursued the invaders, inflicted a sharp defeat on them, and enabled Lot to return safely to his home.

But Sodom and the nearby city of Gomorrah had become evil places, full of sexual perversion and corruption of every kind. No doubt the inhabitants were convinced that morals were what they chose to consider them. No doubt the intellectuals among them proclaimed that God was dead.

But God was not dead. He was watching with growing anger. And eventually the day came when He decided to act.

The Destruction of the Wicked Cities

As the nephew of the upright and God-fearing Abram, Lot was determined not to become involved in the kind of moral degradation that surrounded him. He and his family were the only people in the city of Sodom who feared the Lord and obeyed Him. How long they could have continued to keep up their standards is an interesting question: It's hard to be surrounded by fire and not eventually be burned. Fortunately for Lot, that day had not yet arrived. The inhabitants of Sodom still considered him an outsider;

they were willing to let him go his way so long as they could go theirs.

Meanwhile, over on the plain of Mamre, much was happening in the life of Abram. In material things he continued to prosper, but one thing troubled him greatly: his wife, Sarai, had not given him any children. The Lord assured him that one day Sarai would give him a son and even changed Abram's name to Abraham, which means "father of many." He also changed Sarai's name to Sarah, which means "queen" or "princess."

But the years were passing, both were getting old, and the promised son had not appeared.

At one point, convinced that she would never bear children, Sarah had arranged for her husband to take one of her handmaidens as a concubine. It was not unusual in those days for a barren wife to urge her husband to have children by other women. So Hagar, the Egyptian slave, had had a child by Abraham, a boy named Ishmael. But Hagar took advantage of her new status to make Sarah feel inferior as a woman, and so there was no love lost between them. At one point during Hagar's pregnancy Sarah had become so angry and hostile that the Egyptian woman fled from her into the desert. But an angel of the Lord had told Hagar to go back and have her baby. And so an uneasy peace was established in the household.

One afternoon when Abraham was sitting in the shaded doorway of his tent "in the heat of the day," he looked up and saw three strangers approaching. The law of hospitality among nomadic people in ancient times was very strong (it still is), so Abraham at once invited the travelers to stay with him. He brought water for them to wash their feet, a cool luxury after the burning sands across which they had come. He had Sarah prepare a splendid meal. He spread it before his three guests in the shade of a tree and stood by respectfully while they ate.

Now one of these strangers was the Lord Himself. He knew that Abraham was beginning to fear that Sarah would never have children. So He told His host not to doubt, because a son would indeed be born to them.

Inside the tent, Sarah overheard this prediction and gave a rueful laugh, because she was sure that she was long past childbearing age. The Lord heard her laugh, but instead of being angry, He said a wonderful thing. He said, and I like to think that He smiled as He said it, "Is any thing too hard for the Lord?"

Consider what a marvelous phrase that is! The Bible is full of great thoughts to cling to when we meet difficulties, and this is one of the greatest. It means that no matter how hopeless things seem, there is always someone to turn to, someone so all-wise and all-powerful that in His presence problems simply melt away. Remember that phrase the next time some thorny problem baffles you or some harsh difficulty threatens to overwhelm you. Ask yourself, "Is anything too hard for the Lord?" And then hand the problem over to Him!

Well, to get back to the Bible story, the Lord and His two angels (for such were the other two strangers) were on their way to

Sodom. If the city was as wicked as it was reputed to be, the Lord told Abraham, He was going to destory it.

Abraham tried to dissuade the Lord, pointing out that there might be a few righteous people in Sodom. "To slay the righteous with the wicked," he said, "that be far from thee." This concern of Abraham's for abstract justice and for people he didn't even know is further proof of what a remarkable man he was, and how far ahead of his time. He was, in effect, answering Cain's question: "Am I my brother's keeper?"—answering it in the affirmative.

Patient with Abraham's objections, the Lord finally agreed that if He could find even ten righteous people in Sodom, He would not destroy the city. As it turned out, there were not even ten. The two angel companions of the Lord came to Sodom, stayed in Lot's house, and barely escaped being maltreated by the evil-minded citizens of that evil-minded place. They warned Lot to flee with his wife and family "lest thou be consumed in the iniquity of the city."

Lot's two sons-in-law refused to listen, so the angels took Lot and his wife and his two daughters by the hand, led them out of the city, and told them to escape while they could. They warned them urgently not to turn back or even look back. As the four frightened refugees made their way to a small town called Zoar, the Lord rained fire and brimstone on Sodom and Gomorrah, destroying them utterly, and every living soul in them. Lot and his daughters escaped. But Lot's wife, disobeying the angels, looked back. "And she became a pillar of salt."

A pillar of salt! Perhaps there is a hint here that the salt waters of the Dead Sea rolled over both wicked cities. That desolate region is known for earthquakes, and a violent upheaval of the earth's crust could have done it. If so, the ruins may still lie somewhere beneath that bitter brine. Or perhaps the lesson is simply that those who keep looking back and dwelling on the mistakes and sins of the past are likely to find themselves paralyzed and immobilized so far as moving on into the future is concerned.

In any case, the stern moral message of this great Book of Genesis is once more reaffirmed, the message that man must beware how he uses the gift of free will that has been given to him. Those who love God and revere him, like Noah and Abraham, will be saved. Those who reject and disobey Him, like the people of Sodom and Gomorrah, will suffer the consequences.

The Acid Test

Time passed, and God's promise to Abraham came true: despite her great age, Sarah did have a son. As the Lord commanded, she called him Isaac, which means "he laughs" — a name chosen, perhaps, to remind her of her own lack of faith in the power of the Lord. It was a great day for Abraham, now a hundred years old, when his son and heir was born.

By now Ishmael was in his early teens. All these years he had had his father's love all to himself, so it is likely that he resented the arrival of the new baby. He showed his displeasure by teasing the newcomer, and naturally Sarah resented this. Also, now that

she had a son of her own, Sarah did not want a half brother in the family who might compete for Abraham's affection or even some day contest Isaac's inheritance. So the smoldering animosity between Sarah and Hagar once more burst into flame. Always highly emotional, Sarah now demanded that Abraham banish Hagar and Ishmael from his household permanently.

The old patriarch was unhappy about this, because he loved Ishmael. But he loved Sarah more—or perhaps he was a bit afraid of his wife when her hot temper flared. So he gave in to her. He "rose up early in the morning," gave Hagar some bread and a jar or skin full of water, and sent her and her son away into the desert.

Now the Bible is the greatest of books, full of the greatest stories ever told, but it is also a book that wastes no words. Often it gives just the bare bones of a story, leaving details to the reader's imagination.

For instance, it says of Hagar that "she departed, and wandered in the wilderness." Not a word about the dramatic scenes that must have preceded her banishment. No description of the wilderness itself. The writer of Genesis is relying on the reader to *imagine* what it was like. He is challenging us to visualize this dark Egyptian woman leading her child across the endless sandhills under a blazing sun, doling out the water drop by drop, probably denying herself even the smallest sip, watching the boy droop and wilt, carrying him for a while until her own strength gave out, then placing him under a bush in a pitiful patch of shade. Think of that poor slavewoman's state of mind: not just the dreadful pangs of thirst, but the loneliness of that desolate place, the fear of wild animals, the cruel sense of injustice—after all, in giving Abraham a son she had only done what Sarah wanted her to do—the despair that came upon her when she could go no farther and realized that her only child was dying.

In a few poignant words the writer does tell us that Hagar could not bear to watch Ishmael die. She dragged herself about a hundred yards away—"as it were a bow-shot"—and sat there with her face in her hands and wept.

What was happening now back in Abraham's tent? Again it's left to the imagination of the reader to picture the anxiety that Abraham must have felt, his growing remorse and self-condemnation. He did have the promise of the Lord that Ishmael would survive somehow, but still he must have felt he had done a harsh and cruel thing. And what of Sarah? Did her sense of triumph fade away, leaving her with a guilty conscience? No mother can really wish the death of another woman's child. Perhaps in time she was able to put the Egyptian woman and the child out of her mind. But I doubt that Abraham ever did.

Meanwhile, in the desert, Hagar sat in total despair, convinced that nothing could save her. But, like her enemy Sarah, she was to discover that nothing is too hard for the Lord. The story says that God heard the child crying, and that the angel of God (that is, the aspect of God that deals with human beings directly) called to Hagar. She was told to pick up her child again and hold him in her arms, because the Lord intended to make a great nation out of him. "And God opened her eyes," the narrator says simply, "and she saw a well of water." Probably it was a tiny spring that she had failed to notice in her misery (a message here, too, for those who give up hope too easily: sometimes despair keeps you from seeing the means of your salvation!). So Hagar and Ishmael were saved, and this son of Abraham grew up in the desert, became a skilled hunter with bow and arrow, and finally married a wife who came from Egypt, like his mother. According to tradition, one of his sons was an ancestor of the prophet Muhammud. Thus Muslims consider themselves the spiritual descendants of Abraham to this day.

Young Isaac, however, was growing up under the proud eye of his father. If Abraham had loved Ishmael—and he did—how much more must he have loved this only child of his lawful wife, born by special intervention of the Lord long after such a thing seemed biologically possible.

Love is never ignored in heaven and so Abraham's love for Isaac did not escape God's notice. Now the Lord decided to use that love to make one final and supreme test of Abraham's faith and obedience. He ordered Abraham to take his only son and sacrifice him as a burnt offering on a lonely mountaintop. Bind him like a sheep or a goat. Kill him with a knife with his own hand. Burn the remains on a crude altar. Ask no questions, make no judgments, simply leave the justification of such a dreadful deed to the Lord Himself.

Human sacrifice was common enough in those days, eighteen or nineteen centuries before Christ, but to the gentle Abraham this command must have come like a thunderbolt, incomprehensible, terrifying, appalling

in its injustice and inhumanity. It meant—or seemed to mean—that the God he had served and loved for so long was as ferocious and bloodthirsty as the pagan gods he had always despised. It meant that God, who had promised to make his descendants as numerous as the stars of heaven, was a liar, because if Isaac was killed there would be no such descendants. Abraham had dared to argue with God about the fate of the inhabitants of Sodom, but now apparently he was too stunned to raise his voice. Like Noah, he bowed in blind obedience to the will of God. He saddled his donkey, cut the wood for the burnt offering, took two servants and his young son, and set out for "the place of which God had told him."

What were his thoughts along the way? We can only guess, but they must have been anguished beyond description. How could God command a thing like this? Was it possible or even thinkable to defy or disobey Him? Did the thought cross Abraham's mind, perhaps, that this was a punishment for his own weakness in yielding to Sarah and sending Hagar and his other son out into the desert to perish?

And what were Isaac's thoughts? Did it all seem at first like a pleasant and casual outing into the hills? He was an observant lad. He noticed that his father was carrying a knife, and that wood for an offering was loaded on the donkey. But where was the sacrificial animal? When he asked about this, his father replied patiently that God would provide a lamb when the time came. In this whole moving description of a father willing to sacrifice a beloved son is foreshadowed the great drama and message of the New Testament.

When Abraham left the servants behind and began grimly and silently to climb the mountain with Isaac, the intelligent boy must have known intuitively that something dark and terrible was hanging over them. Certainly he offered no resistance when his father began to bind him with the cords, although by then the full horror of the situation was all too apparent. Perhaps his trust in his father was stronger than his fear. Perhaps he was too frightened to run or to resist. In any case, God tested Abraham right up to the last split second. The sun must have glinted fearfully on the knife as the old man raised it above his son's defenseless throat. Perhaps the sharp edge had even touched the soft skin when the voice of the Lord rang like a great trumpet above those mountaintops: "Abraham, Abraham!"

The old man said, still holding the knife in his shaking hand, "Here am I."

And the Lord told him to release Isaac, "for now I know that thou...hast not withheld thy son, thine only son, from me."

Looking up, Abraham saw a ram with its horns caught in a thicket. He caught the ram and sacrificed it in a gesture of humility and reverence, love and gratitude. To this day, in synagogues on certain high holy days, the rabbi blows a blast on the *shofar*, the ancient ram's horn, to remind the people of the faith and obedience of their ancestor on that lonely mountaintop almost four thousand years ago.

The central message of this great story, one of the most moving and dramatic in the whole Bible, is plain. The message is that if a person will just get his mind full of faith and let the faith thoughts drive out the fear thoughts, all will be well. If that person will let strong belief replace the doubting thoughts, the weakness thoughts in his mind, he will gain enormous strength over all obstacles and difficulties.

That is why reading the Bible is so important. Not just as poetry, not just as history, not just as literature, although it is all those things, but as a reservoir of faith concepts that can release tremendous power in anyone who will use them.

For a fact, if you take a faith thought out of the Bible each day and drive it deep into your mind and dwell on it and nurture yourself on it, gradually you will become an indomitable individual. The sin and weakness and tensions of the world will no longer overwhelm you. You won't be arrogant or conceited, because you will know that your strength isn't generated by you—it comes from God. But you will be a confident, effective, fear-free person.

Why is faith so important? Because it's the greatest of all mind-conditioners. What problem is troubling you right now? What difficulty has you defeated? Whatever it is, the answer is to get your mind freed of the doubt and hesitancy that are keeping it in chains. Whether we succeed or whether we fail in the important things of life is all in the mind. It isn't in the circumstances. It's the thought processes that determine how we deal with the circumstances.

That is what the Bible says over and over again either directly or indirectly, as in this story of Abraham and Isaac. Faith is a form of belief. Belief is a form of thought. All the believing you will ever do is done in the mind. You can either disbelieve yourself into a frustrated life, or you can believe yourself into a great one.

The Bible says it is up to you.

The First
Love Story

The years went by; life's shadows were lengthening around Abraham. He had great possessions, but his beloved wife, Sarah, was dead. He had a son and heir, but Isaac, now a grown man, grieved for his mother and had yet to take a wife. His son's melancholy state of mind troubled the old patriarch. He felt more and more strongly that Isaac needed to have a wife and family of his own.

But Abraham did not want his son to choose a wife from among the Canaanite people in whose land they lived. His own painfully established relationship with God was too precious, too unique to be exposed to any possible pagan influence. It would be far better, Abraham told himself, if Isaac's wife came from his own people, the daughter of a kinsman perhaps. That way his daughter-in-law's religious faith would be strong, her ideals and moral values would be high, she would transmit Isaac's great heritage to their children.

Abraham knew that far to the north in the city of Haran his brother Nahor's family had prospered and grown numerous. Perhaps, he thought, a suitable young woman might be found there. Ordinarily the father of an unmarried son might have sent the young bachelor to a far country to choose a bride for

himself. But Abraham was afraid that if he let Isaac go, the boy might be tempted to remain in Mesopotamia permanently. This was a possibility that filled Abraham with dread, because he knew the Lord wanted him and his descendants to stay in Canaan.

So he called in his most trusted servant— probably it was the same Eliezer mentioned earlier in the Bible who had been his chief steward and overseer for many years. "Swear to me," said Abraham, "that you will go to my brother's home in Haran and seek until you find a bride for my son among his people. If you find such a girl and gain her consent, bring her back with you. If you find her and she refuses to come, then you will be released from your promise."

Eliezer took ten of his master's best camels, loaded them with supplies for the journey and also with valuable gifts, chose some of the bravest and hardiest of Abraham's tribesmen, and began the long trek north.

Swaying across hills and valleys, rivers and deserts, the old servant wondered uneasily how he would be able to recognize the right woman when he found her. As a loyal follower of Abraham, he had great respect for his master's unseen but all-powerful

Deity. And so he did what comes naturally to religious men everywhere when they are faced with a problem: he asked the Lord to help him.

He asked for help in a very specific way. Eliezer knew that in all villages and towns at a certain time of day the young women gathered at the public well to gossip and fill their pitchers. Now he asked the Lord to arrange a meeting for him with such a girl when he came to the city of Haran. "If I ask her for a drink of water," he prayed, "let her give me one. Not only that, let her be so considerate and so kind that without any prompting she will offer to water my camels also. If she does these things, I will take it as a sign from You that she is the girl I am seeking."

Eliezer, in other words, was asking for divine guidance. He believed that the Lord could direct him far better than his own fallible human judgment. And as always happens when someone's faith is strong, the Lord heard him. He brought Rebekah, the granddaughter of Nahor, to the well just as the string of weary camels from Canaan came lurching down the dusty road.

It's one of the most charming scenes in the Bible, the meeting between the graceful girl, "very fair to look upon," with her water pitcher balanced on her shoulder, and the dust-caked, grizzled old family retainer. If feminine beauty had been the only thing that Eliezer was seeking, he would have been satisfied then and there.

But actually the old servant had chosen two yardsticks much more significant: kindness and courage. Not many young girls in those days when all strangers were potential enemies would have heeded a travel-stained wayfarer's request for a drink. Some might have run away. But Rebekah didn't. Smiling, she offered him the brimming pitcher. Then, without being asked, she proceeded to make the much greater effort of drawing water from the deep well for the thirsty animals.

Convinced now that the Lord had guided him to the right person, Eliezer rewarded Rebekah by presenting her with an earring of gold and two heavy gold bracelets. She must have been amazed, but if she was hesitant about accepting such lavish recompense, the Bible doesn't say so. It merely says that she identified herself as Nahor's granddaughter. Then she ran home and breathlessly told her family what had happened.

Rebekah had a brother named Laban, who listened to her story in amazement. This first glimpse of Laban offers us quick insight into his shrewd, somewhat grasping personality. He hurried down to the well and offered hospitality to Abraham's servant. But the Bible tells us, with wry humor perhaps, that it was after "he saw the earring, and bracelets upon his sister's hands."

Regardless of Laban's motives, the visitor from Canaan was given a royal welcome. When he told of his master's great prosperity and opened the packs of rich merchandise to prove it, no one made any objection to his proposal that Rebekah return with him to become Isaac's wife. "Ask the girl herself," they said. "See if she's willing to go." From this ancient passage in the Bible, some authorities think, came the Hebrew tradition that a woman must consent to her own betrothal and her own marriage.

Rebekah was quite willing to go. Perhaps Eliezer's story of how he found her made her feel that this strange proposal was God's will. Perhaps—who knows?—she was bored with the safe routine of life at home, or had found no young man who appealed to her. Behind that pretty face, as we shall see, was a sharp mind and a strong will. She said serenely, "I will go." And that settled that.

It was decided that Rebekah could take her old nurse with her. Perhaps Rebekah wanted one familiar face to keep her from being homesick. Or perhaps, fiercely protective, the old woman insisted on going to guard and care for her mistress in a strange land. In any case, good-byes were said, and the rested camels began the long journey home.

Meantime, was Isaac awaiting his bride

with eagerness and impatience? The Bible doesn't say. Perhaps he had some doubts. After all, this was his father's idea, not his own. What if the girl were ugly? What if she were pious but stupid? Isaac was already forty years old, and we have hints that he was a bit of a mama's boy. We're told that he went out "to meditate in the field at the eventide," and undoubtedly his meditations were a mixture of hopes and fears. While he was meditating, staring at the ground, we're told that "he lifted up his eyes... and, behold, the camels were coming."

Rebekah, too, must have felt her heart beat faster when she saw Isaac at a distance and Eliezer told her who he was. When she heard that it was the man she was to marry, she modestly took a veil and covered her face, so that Isaac's first impression of this bride from a distant land must have been limited to a pair of dark, expressive eyes and a musical, submissive voice, and perhaps the glint of golden bracelets on a slender wrist.

Like all good love stories, this one has a happy ending. Doubts and uncertainties are swept aside. Boy gets girl. Isaac "brought [Rebekah] into his mother Sarah's tent" (at last he had found someone to take his mother's place) "and she became his wife; and he loved her." Interesting how, in this very early romantic story, love follows marriage—it doesn't precede it.

Thus it came about that the lonely Isaac found love—and was comforted.

The Stolen Birthright

Great men usually overshadow their sons, and to some extent this was true in the case of Abraham and Isaac. Certainly Isaac's life seems placid compared to the dramatic career of his father, the wanderer from Ur.

We left Isaac as a happy bridegroom. So far as we know, his marriage to Rebekah was a monogamous one. No additional wives. No concubines. Now we see him twenty years later. Rebekah has had no children, so Isaac petitions the Lord and is rewarded with twin boys. This is the first mention of twins in the Bible, and it marks the beginning of a new set of stormy relationships between these vivid characters who people the pages of Genesis.

The Bible says that even before birth the twins "struggled together" inside their mother's body. The firstborn was named Esau. The second, delivered so quickly after the first that his hand was clutching his brother's foot, was named Jacob, which means "he takes by the heel." It is in such vivid small details that these old stories ring so true.

From the very first breath, these twins were about as different as brothers could be. Rugged and hairy, Esau was a typical outdoorsman, bluff, hearty, quick-tempered, but essentially good-natured and incapable of holding a grudge. Jacob was the scholarly type, thoughtful, intellectual, sensitive, with smooth pale skin quite free of the reddish pelt that covered his brother's muscular body.

As mothers sometimes do, Rebekah favored her younger son. Perhaps his quick mind and sense of humor amused her. Perhaps he preferred his mother to his father—and showed it. Perhaps Rebekah's womanly fastidiousness was repelled by Esau's crude manners and lusty behavior. Perhaps she truly thought that Jacob was better fitted by brains and temperament to be the leader of God's people. The Bible tells us that both she and Isaac were disturbed when, in his lusty, earthy way, Esau took two wives from the Hittite women among whom Isaac's family lived.

In any case, Rebekah made up her mind to push Jacob ahead of Esau one way or another. And eventually she did.

Jacob had already taken one step in that direction himself, by talking his older brother out of the birthright that entitled Esau, as the firstborn, to a double share of family possessions. One day when Esau came back half-starved from hunting, he found Jacob preparing a delicious meal of lentils. When Esau asked for a portion, Jacob coolly replied that he could have it if he would surrender his birthright to him. The impatient Esau agreed. "What good is my birthright to me," he cried, "if I starve to death?" So, as the Bible puts it, he "despised his birthright" and traded it for a helping of red pottage made of lentils.

The underlying message here seems plain indeed. It is that all worthwhile achievements—and ultimately civilization itself—

rest on man's willingness to postpone immediate pleasures or benefits in favor of greater future rewards. In any life, this kind of self-discipline is essential. Obviously Esau didn't have it, whereas Jacob did. It's altogether possible that when she heard of this foolish and impetuous act, Rebekah made up her mind then and there that Esau was not worthy of becoming a patriarch.

Now Isaac, on the other hand, had always preferred his older boy. A gentle person himself, he was impressed by Esau's energy and strength and skill at hunting. He also liked to eat the wild game that Esau brought home so frequently. As he grew older, and as his eyesight failed, eating became one of the few pleasures left to Isaac. So one day, knowing that his own death might not be far

off, he asked Esau to go hunting, bring back some venison, prepare it the way his father liked it, and receive the formal blessing that would symbolize the transfer of authority from one generation to the next.

"And Rebekah heard," the Bible says— eavesdropping, actually—and she knew that she had to move quickly or the leadership of the tribe would be lost to Jacob forever. So she told Jacob to bring her two kids from the flock. She would prepare a meal that would fool her husband into thinking that Esau had brought home the venison. Jacob was to take it in to his blind father, pretend to be Esau, and receive the promised blessing.

Jacob seems to have had few scruples about this deception, but he was afraid of

being found out. He pointed out that his father might touch him and recognize his smooth skin. What if this happened and his father cursed him instead of blessing him? That would be a terrible and terrifying thing.

But like so many women in the Bible, Rebekah could dominate the men around her. "Do as I say," she told Jacob fiercely. "If anything goes wrong, I'll take the curse upon myself!"

So Jacob did exactly as she told him. He put on some of Esau's clothes, clothes that—as any modern hunter's wife will tell you often happens—had a distinctive aroma of their own. She made him cover the back of his neck and his hands with the hairy skin of the young kids. Then she made him take the steaming dish into his father's tent.

One amazing thing about the Bible is the way it refuses to pull any punches where its heroes are concerned. In this amazing scene Jacob appears as an out-and-out liar. Not only that, he involves the Lord in his lies. When Isaac, suspicious and puzzled, asks how the venison could have been obtained so quickly, Jacob replies smoothly that the Lord brought him good luck.

Still unconvinced, the old man insists on touching the boy. The hairy skin of the goats leaves him more puzzled still. "The voice," he murmurs to himself, "is Jacob's voice, but the hands are the hands of Esau." So he asks a direct question: "Are you really my son Esau?"

By now Jacob is very frightened, but he is in too deep to back out. As usually happen with liars, one lie inevitably leads to more lies. "I am," he says defiantly. His father draws him close, kisses him, smells the rugged outdoors smell of Esau's clothing, and is convinced. He gives his blessing to Jacob.

Almost at once, Esau comes back from the field and brings his dish of venison to his father. "Who are you?" asks the old man in his quavering voice. "Your son," is the reply, "your firstborn, Esau!"

Then, says the Bible in a vivid and poignant phrase, "Isaac trembled very exceedingly," because he knew he had been tricked. And when Esau heard what had happened, he cried "with a great and exceeding bitter cry": "Bless me, even me also, O my father!"

But the blessing, once given, could not be retracted. Rebekah's plot had succeeded. Now Jacob, not Esau, would be the spiritual leader of Abraham's descendants.

In his rage, Esau vowed to kill his brother. When she heard of this, Rebekah decided to send Jacob to her brother, Laban, far to the north in Mesopotamia. Jacob could stay there until Esau's rage had cooled. Jacob, terrified of his brother, agreed to go. Rebekah thought that her favorite son would soon return, but she was wrong, and this was the penalty that she paid for her deceit. It was twenty years before Jacob returned. By that time, his mother was dead.

The Shining Ladder

It must have been a troubled and disconsolate Jacob who left his father's home and began the long journey to Haran, where sanctuary awaited him with his mother's people. Apparently he traveled alone, so he must have had time for some somber thoughts. He had talked his brother into giving up his birthright and he had gained his father's blessing by trickery, but it's unlikely that he was very happy about these two tainted triumphs. Perhaps he tried, as he walked along, to find excuses for himself. Perhaps he said, as his ancestor Adam once had said, "The woman tempted me...," the woman in this case being his mother. How easy it is, when people have done wrong, for them to convince themselves that the fault was someone else's!

In any case, the lonely traveler "lighted upon a certain place, and tarried there all night, because the sun was set." He made a hard, lonely pillow out of some stones he found and lay down to sleep. "And he dreamed, and behold a ladder set up on the earth, and the top of it reached to heaven." It seemed to Jacob in this vision that angels were ascending and descending this ladder, and at the top stood the Lord Himself. If God was angry with Jacob, He didn't show it. On the contrary. He promised to be with him always and eventually to bring him back to this land which he was fleeing.

Jacob woke terrified, as men who have a guilty conscience often do. The dream was so vivid that he was sure that somehow he had come upon a place where the veil between the natural and the supernatural was very thin. And perhaps it was. Who is to say that God doesn't speak to us through dreams when the conscious mind—that is, the arrogant, self-willed part of us—is asleep?

When he awoke, Jacob began to do some hard praying, which was probably something he hadn't done in a long time. If he had been praying regularly, I doubt if he would have been able to lie to his father so readily: prayers and lies somehow just don't go together. Now the frightened and penitent Jacob told the Lord that if He would just stay with him and keep him safe and bring him home again someday, he would acknowledge Him as his God (this implies that Jacob hadn't been doing so lately!); not only that, he would give the Lord a tenth of whatever worldly goods he might ever possess. This is the first mention in the Bible of tithing, a spiritual discipline that is just as valid and effective today as it was then.

Dreams have always fascinated people, and this dream of Jacob's is no exception. What did it mean? What does the image of a great ladder stretched between earth and heaven imply?

Does it not mean that no matter where a person may be, no matter how desolate the place, no matter how lonely or discouraged he is, no matter how stained he may be with sin or falsehood or deceit, the channel is always open for him to communicate with God? There is always a golden ladder with man at one end and God at the other, and that ladder is the thing we call prayer.

Perhaps, as the dream implied, only angels constantly live and move on this spiritual plane. But man can be a part of it. Man can make contact with it. Man can put his foot on the bottom rung of the ladder whenever he wants to, and God, who is at the

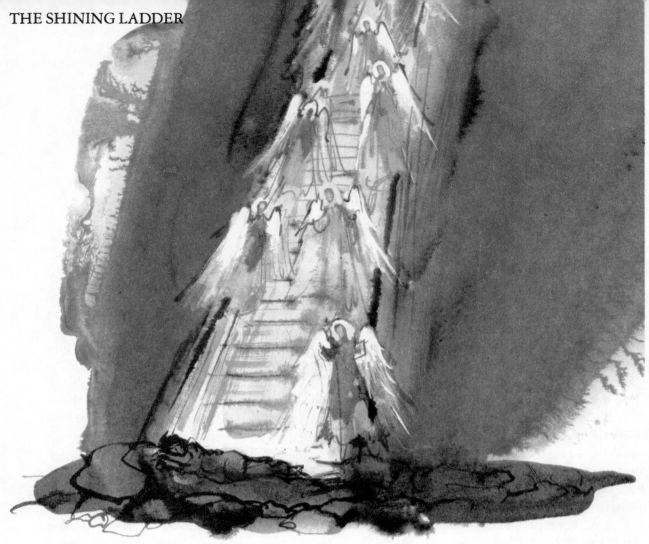

top, will know it and be responsive to him.

This vision of Jacob's has been the inspiration for much art and much music. The old hymn *Nearer, My God, to Thee* makes reference to it:

> *Though, like the wanderer,*
> *the sun gone down,*
> *Darkness comes over me,*
> *my rest a stone,*
> *Yet in my dreams I'd be*
> *Nearer, My God, to Thee. . . .*

The author of that hymn felt a spiritual kinship with Jacob, and so do we all. All men, whether they know it or not, are seeking some kind of ladder to lead them to God.

Anyone who reads or hears this story of Jacob's ladder might well consider this proposition: what would hapen to you, and through you to the world, if you were to make the practice of prayer a central program in your life? What do you think would happen if, instead of hurriedly skimming through a book like this, you actually saturated your mind with the Bible itself, actually studied and practiced the principles of prayer that it contains? Of course, most of us pray, to some extent, but doubtless most of us would admit that most of the time we only dabble in it.

If a person went all out in a thoroughgoing prayer program, it would be the most revolutionary, life-changing, tremendous experience that person ever had. If you were that person, problems that now baffle you would be solved, burdens that weigh you down would become lighter, sickness or illness that cripples you would be met with power. Tremendous things would happen.

"More things are wrought by prayer," wrote the poet Tennyson, "than this world dreams of." Almost the last words of the great scientist Charles Steinmetz to his colleagues in the laboratories were, "Prayer—find out about prayer!"

Jacob found out about it by using it. That was more than thirty centuries ago, but the power is still there. We can use it too.

The Return of the Exile

Awe-stricken but also heartened by his vision, Jacob came safely to Haran and found shelter with his mother's brother, Laban. Laban's offer of asylum was all the more welcome because there was in his household a beautiful young girl named Rachel. Actually, Laban had two daughters. The Bible tells us that Leah, the older one, was "tender-eyed," which sounds romantic but actually means that Leah's eyes were weak. Perhaps she was nearsighted. Or perhaps was cross-eyed. From the start Leah was attracted by the handsome young refugee from Canaan. But Jacob lost his heart to the beautiful Rachel.

Still as shrewd and grasping as ever, Laban quickly realized that the bright and energetic Jacob could be a useful addition to his household, especially when it came to building up his herds, the chief measure of a man's wealth in those days. What, he asked, would Jacob want in the way of wages to stay and work for him? Lovesick and starry-eyed, Jacob said that all he wanted was Rachel's hand in marriage. He offered to serve seven years without pay if at the end of that time he could claim her as his bride.

Crafty Laban was no man to turn down such a bargain. He accepted with alacrity and proceeded to work his nephew hard. But hard work meant nothing to Jacob so long as he could be close to his beloved. The Bible, compressing so much into so few words as it often does, tells us that the seven years "seemed unto him but a few days, for the love he had to her."

Finally the longed-for wedding day came. Laban gave a lavish feast for all his retainers. That evening, in accordance with the traditional ritual, he brought his daughter, heavily veiled, to the bridegroom's tent. But the silent, veiled figure was not the daughter that Jacob was expecting. When daylight came, the astonished and dismayed bridegroom discovered that Laban had brought him not Rachel but Leah.

Furious, Jacob demanded an explanation of such trickery. "Oh," said the wily Laban, "in this country it's our custom never to give a younger daughter in marriage until her older sister has a husband. I thought you knew!"

There was nothing Jacob could do about it. He agreed to serve Laban another seven years without pay if he could marry Rachel as well. Thus both daughters of Laban became Jacob's wives.

Jacob's preference for Rachel was so strong, and he showed it so plainly, that the Lord felt sorry for Leah and allowed her to bear children while Rachel had none. Each time Leah had a son the unhappy woman said to herself, "Now at last my husband will love me." But all her faithful childbearing earned her was the jealousy and enmity of her sister.

When Rachel saw that she could not become pregnant, she gave her maid, Bilhah, to Jacob as a concubine, just as Sarah had given Hagar to Abraham two generations earlier. Later Leah did the same thing with her servant Zilpah. As the years went by, Jacob acquired a family of ten boys and a girl.

During these years Rachel suffered greatly, because to be childless was considered a disgrace. Finally the Lord heard her prayers and allowed her to conceive and bear a son. "God hath taken away my reproach," she said happily, and she named the child Joseph.

After Joseph was born, Jacob wanted to return to his father's home in Canaan. But Laban, who rightly attributed his own prosperity to Jacob's skill in managing the herds, begged him not to go. Jacob finally agreed to stay if he could have for his own all the brown lambs among the sheep and all the speckled or spotted goats. Since such animals were comparatively rare, Laban quickly agreed. But now the trickster became the tricked. Jacob had so much knowledge of animal husbandry that he was able to breed the herds so that great numbers of brown

sheep and spotted goats were born. Soon his flocks were greater than Laban's.

This led to great resentment among Laban's sons, who felt that Jacob was robbing them of their inheritance. Their hostility increased until Jacob began to fear for the safety of himself and his family. So one day, without giving any notice to Laban, he "rose up, and set his sons and his wives upon camels; and he carried away all his cattle, and all the goods which he had gotten... for to go to Isaac his father in the land of Canaan."

This was the second time that Jacob had fled along the caravan trail between Canaan and Mesopotamia, leaving an angry relative behind. Finding both his daughters and his

son-in-law gone, Laban pursued them and overtook Jacob's household after a week of hard marching. But the Lord warned him in a dream not to harm Jacob or to try to make him turn back. So the two descendants of Terah made their peace and parted in friendship.

Jacob continued his journey, but now he was oppressed by the thought of meeting Esau again. Twenty years had passed, but Jacob knew that some men have long memories. Esau was probably still the rough, impetuous man of action that he had always been. What if he were still angry? What if he were still determined to kill his brother—kill not only him but his whole family as well? The closer Jacob came to Canaan, the more worried he grew. He sent messengers ahead to tell Esau that he was coming. The messengers returned with the ominous news that Esau was marching north with four hundred men. Just that word and nothing more. Jacob began to pray more fervently than he had in some time.

Just as Jacob had had a strange and mystical experience on his way to Haran when he dreamed of the ladder, now he was to have one equally strange on his way home. At a place where the river Jabbok was shallow, he sent his family and his retainers across, but he himself stayed behind. While he was alone, during the night, a stranger appeared, a powerful being in the likeness of a man and yet somehow not a man. The apparition grappled with Jacob, wrestled with him all night long, and put his thighbone out of joint. When daybreak came, the stranger struggled to get away, but Jacob refused to release him until his opponent had given him his blessing. The apparition told Jacob that henceforth he would be called Israel, which means "champion of God," "soldier of God," or "He who strives with God." But he would not give his own name, and after blessing Jacob, he disappeared.

Who or what was this strange apparition? A modern psychologist might point out that Jacob was under a lot of pressure, that he was indeed wrestling with a problem—the problem of whether to face his brother or run away again. Also, the insistence on a blessing might be a guilt echo of the trickery whereby Jacob had obtained his own father's blessing.

And yet the episode must have been more than just another dream, because when Jacob crossed the river the next day he was lame from the injury to his thigh. Jacob himself was convinced that the stranger was God Himself. "I have seen God face to face," he said, "and my life is preserved." Martin Luther once suggested that the antagonist might have been the "pre-existent Christ," and that it was actually Jesus who thus visited Jacob hundreds of years before the Nativity in Bethlehem.

Be that as it may, Jacob went forth the next day to meet his brother. Far off on the horizon he saw a cloud of dust where Esau was coming with his four hundred men. Calmly Jacob arranged his family in a procession with the concubines and their children in front, then Leah and her children, and finally the two he loved most, Rachel with young Joseph, at the rear where they would have the most protection. Then he walked past them, bowing to the ground seven times in great humility as he approached his brother.

It was a moment of agonizing suspense for the travelers from Haran. But then, in a scene that foreshadows the great story of the Prodigal Son, instead of trying to kill his brother, the good-hearted Esau "ran to meet him, and embraced him, and fell on his neck, and kissed him: and they wept." Esau didn't even want to accept the lavish presents that Jacob offered him; he said that he had enough cattle already. But finally, mainly to ease his brother's conscience, he did.

So Jacob returned to the land of his father, but sorrow came with him. In the last stages of the journey Rachel, pregnant for the second time, died in childbirth. The baby, the last of Jacob's sons was called Benjamin. From these twelve sons were to come the twelve tribes of Israel. And the descendants of Jacob are known as the children of Israel to this day.

From Prisoner to Prince

Of all his children old Israel—or Jacob as he was still called by his family—loved Joseph best. The children of Leah were his offspring; so were the sons of the concubines. But Joseph was the first-born of the woman he loved. Benjamin was also Rachel's child, and Jacob loved him dearly too. But Benjamin's birth had cost his mother her life. No, Joseph was the old man's favorite, and everyone knew it.

He was a bright and handsome child. In looks he probably resembled his beautiful mother. And even at an early age he showed some of the drive and determination and energy of his father. But when we first get a close look at Joseph as a youngster of seventeen, he is not a lovable person. He was his father's pet, just as Jacob had once been his mother's pet (family patterns often tend to repeat themselves), and he knew it. In other words, he was spoiled, By and large his older brothers were a rough, self-centered lot. When they made a mistake, or got out of line, Joseph was quite capable of running to tell his father. Nothing escaped his sharp, inquisitive eyes. This did not endear him to his brothers.

Nor did the special garments that his doting father gave him to wear. In the King James version of the bible, it's "a coat of many colors." The Revised Standard Version calls it "a coat with long sleeves." Perhaps it was both. Among those ancient people an ornamented tunic was the sign of a chieftain or leader. Since Joseph ranked only eleventh in age among Jacob's twelve sons, his older brothers saw no reason why he sould be rated ahead of them.

Besides, Joseph had an exasperating way of rubbing it in. "Let me tell you about a dream I had," he said eagerly one morning to his brothers. "We were all in a field together, binding grain into sheaves, and guess what? All your sheaves bowed down to my sheaf! What do you think of that?"

The brothers let him know profanely what they thought, but this did not prevent the brash youngster from relating another dream, one that showed him in an almost godlike position. In this dream, the sun, the moon, and eleven stars were bowing down to Joseph. Even his indulgent father took exception to that kind of egotism and scolded him for it. But being a man of dreams himself, old Jacob wondered privately if prophecy might not be involved in Joseph's dreams as well as conceit.

The resentment of the older brothers smoldered steadily. One day when they were all away tending their father's flocks near a town called Dothan, Jacob sent Joseph to check up on them. Seeing him coming, gay and unconcerned in his coat of many colors (and also exempt from the monotonous work of tending sheep), the brothers felt their anger boil over. "Here comes that wretched dreamer," they said to one another. "Let's get rid of him once and for all. Let's kill him and pretend some wild beast has devoured him. That will put an end to his obnoxious dreams!"

They would have killed him then and

there if the eldest brother, Reuben, had not shown a flicker of compassion. "Let's just throw him in a pit," he said. Actually, what Reuben had in mind was to rescue Joseph later and thus gain the gratitude and favor of his father. But the other brothers liked this method of elimination that seemed to stop short of open murder. They seized Joseph and stripped off his hated coat of many colors. Then, ignoring his frightened cries and pleas for mercy, they threw him into a deep pit, perhaps a dry well, that was nearby.

What a 'shock for an impressionable seventeen-year-old! Walking along one minute in the sunshine, cheerful, gay, enjoying his high opinion of himself and his favored position in life. Then the next minute stripped, bruised, dazed by harsh words and oaths from his own kinsmen, half-stunned

by the fall into a dark and terrifying hole that for all he knew would become his grave. No matter how he screamed, no one would hear him in that lonely place except his brothers, who were now sitting down to eat, filled with the fierce satisfaction of rough, wild men who think they have settled an ancient grudge.

As the brothers ate, along came a caravan of Ishmaelites bound for Egypt, "their camels bearing spicery and balm and myrrh." Then up spoke Judah, another of the brothers. Either his conscience was troubling him, or else he saw a chance to make some easy money. "Why don't we sell Joseph to these merchants?" he said. "They can resell him at a profit in Egypt. That way his blood won't be on our hands, but we'll be rid of him forever."

By now the brothers' anger had cooled somewhat and they had lost their appetite for murder. They hauled Joseph out of the pit, haggled for a while with the fierce, hawk-faced leader of the caravan, and finally sold their brother into slavery for twenty pieces of silver.

That got rid of Joseph, but now there arose the problem of what to tell their father. The solution they hit upon was even crueler than the truth would have been because it denied the old man the knowledge that his favorite son was still alive. The brothers took the coat of many colors, dipped it in the blood of a young kid, then brought the stained garment to their father. "We found this," they said, pretending doubt as to its ownership. "Does it belong to your son or not?"

Poor old Jacob did not doubt this "evidence" that Joseph had been killed by some wild animal. Crushed and despairing, he "mourned for his son many days." The Bible says that all his sons and daughters tried to comfort him, the daughters with sincerity because they did not know the truth, the sons with sickening hypocrisy because they did. But he refused to be comforted. "I will go to my grave," he said pathetically, "mourning for my son."

Meantime, far away in Egypt, the Ishmaelites put Joseph on the auction block where slaves were sold. There must have been some eager bidders for the handsome but dejected lad. It took a rich man to outbid the others, and a rich man—or perhaps his representative—did. When the sun went down that day, Joseph found himself the property of an Egyptian named Potiphar, one of the great Pharoah's most trusted officers, the captain of the royal guard.

What, by this time, was Joseph's state of mind? The Bible story does not tell us, but already he must have been vastly changed from the spoiled, vain youth who left his father's home so lightheartedly to pay a visit to his sheep-tending brothers. As the old saying goes, there's no school like the school of hard knocks for bringing out the latent characteristics in a person. On the long, hard journey down to Egypt, Joseph had had a clear-cut choice: to give in to despair and become a slave in mind and heart as well as in fact, or to summon up all his courage and resourcefulness, trust in God, and wait for a chance to escape from the trap that had closed on him.

This choice was really a gift from God, as hard choices often are. Jacob would never have put his favorite son to such a test. He would have gone on spoiling him indefinitely, and much more spoiling might have ruined the boy. This is a thought that many overprotective parents would do well to ponder: when hardship descends on a child, it may be a blessing in disguise.

In any case, the best qualities in Joseph—patience, intelligence, energy, adaptability—now began to emerge. He quickly learned the language of his master. With astonishing speed he absorbed everything in the more advanced Egyptian culture that was worth absorbing. His quick mind and pleasing personality captivated Potiphar, who gave him more and more freedom and responsibility. Before long the nimble-minded young Hebrew was in charge of the whole household. And just as Jacob's skill and knowledge had benefited Laban a generation earlier, so his son's intelligence and organizing ability brought prosperity to the house of Potiphar.

In refusing to give in to discouragement or despair, Joseph had passed the first real test of his young life, but now an even more difficult one appeared in the form of his master's wife. There is no actual description of this lady in the Genesis story, but we don't need one to visualize her: rich, selfish, bored, arrogant, accustomed to having whatever she wanted whenever she wanted it. Perhaps her husband's military duties caused him to neglect her. Perhaps he was much older than she. Perhaps she made a game of collecting lovers. If so, she decided to add Joseph to her list. She told him that she wanted him to make love to her.

It was a tremendous temptation for the young man. The Ten Commandments had yet to be formulated. He had no wife of his own. Here was a passionate and no doubt elegant woman throwing herself at him. Accepting her proposition might give him a kind of revenge on the Egyptians who looked down on all foreigners, especially Hebrews. Becoming her lover might lead to all sorts of material advantages and privileges. Through Joseph's mind must have run all the rationalizations that participants in adultery ask themselves today. Who will ever find out? What people don't know doesn't hurt them. What's wrong with a little excitement now and then? And so on.

But three things made Joseph refuse the advances of Potiphar's wife. The first was a sense of loyalty and obligation to her husband. This man had trusted and befriended him; how could he now deceive and betray him? The second was his own conscience. "How then," he said to the lustful woman, "can I do this great wickedness?" The third was his belief in a God to whom such actions were a violation of righteousness. That was the ultimate yardstick: the righteousness of God, and it was not a yardstick that could be bent or altered to suit man's convenience.

Joseph tried to make the Egyptian's wife see that what she was proposing was not just a crime against her husband, it was a sin against God. But, probably because she didn't acknowledge a single Supreme Being, she would not listen. She continued in every way to try to seduce Joseph, who in turn tried to avoid her. Then one day the inevitable happened. Furious at being rebuffed, she told her husband that Joseph had made advances to her. This lie so angered Potiphar that he had Joseph thrown into prison.

But think about this for a minute! In a way, mere imprisonment was an act of leniency on the part of this high Egyptian officer who could have ordered Joseph killed on the spot. Perhaps he knew his wife better than she supposed he did. Be that as it may, Joseph was disgraced and imprisoned, but he wasn't put to death.

Once more Joseph might have been justified in giving way to despair, but once again he didn't. He won the confidence of the jailer, who put him in charge of other

prisoners (this Joseph was what we moderns call a "take-charge guy"!). Among the men languishing in jail were two of Pharaoh's servants who had incurred their royal master's anger. Joseph amazed them by interpreting some dreams they had had. He predicted that Pharaoh's butler would be pardoned, but that his baker would be executed. Both predictions came true: the butler was restored to his position in the royal household, but the baker was hanged. One would think that the butler would have remembered the remarkable young Hebrew with gratitude, or even tried to help him. But the Bible says, laconically, that he "forgat him."

Time passed. Joseph remained in prison. Then one night the great Pharaoh, supreme ruler of Egypt, had a pair of disturbing dreams. In the first, seven fat cows were devoured by seven lean ones. In the second, seven plump ears of corn were swallowed up by seven withered ears. Puzzled and somewhat frightened, the monarch summoned his soothsayers and magicians to interpret

the dream. When none could, the butler suddenly remembered Joseph. So the young Hebrew, bathed and shaven, was brought from the prison and placed before the great king.

Many painters have tried to depict the scene with the brooding monarch scowling suspiciously at the tall young man. "I am told that you can interpret dreams," Pharaoh finally said.

"No," replied Joseph, "I have no such power of myself. But God does, and speaking through me, God will give Pharoah a peaceful answer to the dreams that are troubling him."

Who was this ancient monarch? Historians are not sure, but some think it may have been Ikhnaton, the first of the pharaohs

to grasp the concept of monotheism and try to establish it as the religion of his people. The attempt failed; after Ikhnaton's death, the people turned again to their old pagan gods. But it's fascinating to wonder if Ikhnaton and Joseph did meet and, in that case, if Joseph's strong belief in the God of his fathers was somehow related to this momentary flash of spiritual insight that briefly illuminated the dark night of paganism in Egypt so many centuries ago.

Joseph explained to Pharaoh that his dreams were a forewarning of a great famine. There would be seven years of good harvests followed by seven years of drought. He urged the ruler to build granaries and to store surplus food during the good years so that Egypt would survive the lean ones.

Pharaoh was impressed. He not only believed Joseph, he decided to make him director of the whole food program. He put a gold chain around the former prisoner's neck, placed his own ring on his finger, gave him a magnificent chariot to ride in, and ordered all the people to bow down to him. Interestingly, I'm told that an ancient Theban painting has been discovered showing Ikhnaton decorating a young prince with a golden chain because "he had filled up the storehouses" of the land.

From prisoner to prince almost overnight—an extraordinary accomplishment for a young man still only thirty years old. Pharaoh gave Joseph a priest's daughter to marry and made him governor of all the people of Egypt. Two sons were born to him. During the seven years of good harvests, grain piled up in the granaries until it was "as the sand of the sea." Every aspect of Joseph's life was filled with magnificence and fulfillment, but the arrogance that had marred his character and flawed his early youth did not come back. It did not come back because Joseph no longer gave himself credit for all his success.

He gave the credit to God.

The Testing of the Brothers

After the good years, as Joseph had predicted, came the lean ones. Famine haunted the land, not only in Egypt but all through the neighboring countries. In Canaan the crops failed, grazing animals died from lack of pasturage, people were facing starvation. Joseph's brothers, simple-minded herdsmen, had no solution to offer. They shook their heads, scanned the pitiless sky, and muttered that sooner or later it must rain.

Their father, Jacob, was old now, but he was still a man of action, a leader capable of making decisions. "Why do you stand around staring at one another?" he demanded angrily of his sons. "I have heard that there is food to be had in Egypt. Go down there and buy some, before we all perish of hunger!"

The ten brothers did as they were told. They would have taken Benjamin with them, but Jacob would not let them. He had already lost one of Rachel's two sons, or so he thought. He did not want to risk losing another.

When the brothers arrived, they found that they had to obtain permission to buy grain from the all-powerful governor of Egypt. In this mighty personage they did not recognize the kinsman they had sold into slavery so long ago. But Joseph recognized them instantly. He remembered, too, when they bowed humbly before him, the dream of the sheaves of wheat bowing down to his sheaf.

But Joseph did not identify himself for several reasons. First he wanted to know if his father and his younger brother were still alive. Next he wanted to learn if his brothers felt any remorse for the way they had treated him. Finally he wanted them to prove to him, somehow, that they were no longer fierce, selfish men, that the years had mellowed them and taught them the meaning of compassion.

So he spoke to them harshly, accusing them of being foreign spies. When they protested that they were honest buyers of grain whose father and youngest brother were anxiously awaiting their return, Joseph felt a great yearning to see Benjamin once more, his only full brother, the only guiltless one. He told the others sternly that he doubted their story and would hold one of them hostage until they brought Benjamin to see him. If they did, he would believe their story. If not, he would know they were liars.

Consternation prevailed among the brothers at their strange treatment from this awe-inspiring man. Their guilty consciences whispered that this misfortune had come upon them because of their cruel treatment of their brother so many years ago. Reuben, the eldest, even said, "I told you so!" little dreaming that this mighty Egyptian prince who stood so haughtily by could understand every word they were speaking in their native tongue.

The brothers were too afraid of Joseph to question his decree. They agreed to leave Simeon behind as a hostage. Then they loaded their donkeys with the grain that the governor permitted them to buy, and they started home.

On the way they got another shock. One of them opened a sack of grain to feed his donkey. There in the mouth of the sack was a bundle of money equivalent to the amount he had paid for the grain in Egypt! Each man looked; each man found his money where Joseph had secretly ordered his servants to hide it.

It's probable that Joseph was trying to spare his father the expenditure of these funds, but it's also likely that he was paying his brothers back a little by mystifying and frightening them. Men of guilty conscience cannot accept a simple act of charity without wondering if hidden strings are attached. Joseph knew they would be more terrified than pleased. And they were.

Old Jacob's distress was pitiful when he learned that Simeon was a hostage in Egypt and that the great governor there was demanding to see Benjamin. At first he simply refused to let his youngest go. But as the famine worsened and when "they had eaten up the corn which they had brought out of Egypt," there was little choice. The brothers made plans to go back to Egypt, this time taking Benjamin with them.

Old Israel, practical as always, urged them to try to placate the governor. "Take... the man a present," he said, "a little balm, and a little honey, spices and myrrh, nuts and almonds." He also urged them to take a double amount of money in case their money had been returned the first time by mistake. But finally, and typically, he turned to the ultimate source of all help. "And God Almighty give you mercy before the man," he said in his quavering voice, "that he may send away your other brother, and Benjamin."

Apprehensively the brothers retraced their steps along the dusty caravan trail, seeing everywhere the misery caused by the famine, not knowing what awaited them at the end of their journey. Their fears grew with every mile. Would they all be imprisoned for theft? Was Simeon still alive? Would they ever see their father again?

When Joseph ordered them to come to his house for a meal, the invitation left them more frightened than ever, but they spread out the presents they had brought and waited to see what would happen. When the great governor strode into the room, resplendent in his robes of office, they all prostrated themselves before him. But when Joseph saw Benjamin among them, he was so touched that for a moment he could play-act

no longer. Deeply moved, he went into his private quarters where no one could see his tears. It is a poignant scene, this older brother yearning over a younger one, because in the Bible story so far no such emotion has been shown. There has been the love of God for man, and of man for God. There has been the love of man for woman, and of husband for wife. But between brothers, up to now, we have encountered mostly jealousy and hostility, treachery and animosity. Here for the first time the love of brother for brother shines through with unmistakable warmth and feeling. And notice the first words that Joseph addresses to Benjamin: "God be gracious unto thee, my son." Pronouncing this blessing so shook Joseph's iron self-control that he had to leave the room quickly in order to hide his tears.

Soon, though, he recovered. He "washed his face, and went out, and refrained himself"—that is, he mastered his emotions. He sat down alone to eat, as befitted the viceroy of a great kingdom, but he sent portions of food to all his brothers, the largest going to Benjamin. He also seated them in order of seniority, which must have astonished them greatly. How could this man know such things about them? He must be a wizard or a magician, as well as a governor.

Joseph had yet to hear any convincing expression of remorse from his brothers, so he continued his cat-and-mouse game. Once again he sent them away laden with grain, but this time he ordered his servants to conceal his own drinking cup, an ornate silver goblet in Benjamin's sack. Then he sent his steward galloping after them, his chariot wheels stirring up clouds of dust, to accuse them of theft, arrest them, and bring them back. When once more they stood before him, frightened and confused, he told them that he intended to keep Benjamin as his slave and let the others go.

Then at last Judah spoke up bravely. He said that if they returned to Canaan without Benjamin, their father would die of grief. He offered to become a slave himself if only the governor would let Benjamin go. What a change had come over these men! Once they heartlessly sold a brother into slavery; now one of them was ready to become a slave in order to save a brother. The Bible message here is that there is a spark of nobility even in the worst of men; that no human being, however cruel, is entirely beyond hope; that one redeeming act of kindness can go far toward compensating for past mistakes, even though it may not wipe them out.

This urgent plea of Judah's convinced Joseph that his brothers truly were changed men. He sent all his Egyptian servants and retainers out of the room. Then his emotions overcame him and he burst into tears. "I am Joseph," he said to his brothers. "Is my father still alive?"

Fright, guilt, astonishment left the brothers speechless. One can almost see the expression of stupefaction on their faces. Joseph saw it too, but then he said a remarkable thing. He told his brothers not to be ashamed or angry with themselves, because even in their cruelty and heart-

lessness God had been using them to work out His purpose. "It was not you that sent me hither," Joseph said, "but God." What a man! It takes a fine person to sense remorse in people who have wronged him and to give them credit for feeling such remorse. It takes a deeply religious person to see or sense in apparent affliction the mysterious workings of God. This man was both.

The gentle prince sent his brothers home, all eleven of them, to "tell my father of all my glory in Egypt," and to offer him and all his family a home in the land of Goshen, a long, narrow valley on the frontiers of Egypt. When his sons came home bearing their extraordinary news, Jacob's old heart almost stopped beating, because it was almost too good to be true. But when he saw the wagonloads of gifts that Joseph had sent, and the three hundred pieces of silver that he had given to Benjamin, his doubts vanished. "It is enough," said the old patriarch. "Joseph my son is yet alive: I will go and see him before I die."

Overjoyed though he was, the old man wondered if God really wanted him to leave the land of Canaan. So the Lord came to him in a dream and reassured him, saying, "Fear not to go down into Egypt; for...I will go down with thee into Egypt; and I will also surely bring thee up again." So Jacob assembled all the members of his family and moved them to Egypt in the wagons that Pharaoh had provided. There at last he met his long-lost son. Joseph came up to Goshen to meet him, and embraced his father, and "wept on his neck a good while." Later Joseph introduced his father to Pharaoh himself, and the old man blessed this pagan ruler who had heaped so many honors on his son. For seventeen more years Jacob lived peacefully in Goshen, where Joseph could visit him often. He died finally at the age of a hundred and forty-seven. But before he died he made his son promise to bury him with his ancestors in the land of Canaan, and Joseph did.

When their father died, Joseph's older brothers were afraid that he might have been concealing a grudge all this time. They sent him a message saying that their father had specifically left word that they should be forgiven.

The Bible says that when Joseph heard this message he wept. Why these tears? Was he disheartened because, after all his kindness, his brothers still feared him? Was he grieving because, after all he had done, their guilty consciences still tormented them? Whatever the cause, he made a noble reply. "Fear not," he said, "for am I in the place of God?" Who am I, Joseph seems to be saying, to judge my fellow man? Who can read the secrets of the human mind or unravel the motivations of the human heart? Only God can do this. Why not leave it all to Him? Centuries later a Person far greater than Joseph woiuld say the same thing: *Judge not, that ye be not judged....*

So the sons of Jacob were allowed to live in peace in the land of Goshen. Under Joseph's protection, the numbers of their descendants increased greatly. Joseph himself lived to be a hundred and ten. No doubt he could have been buried in Egypt with great pomp and ceremony. No doubt he could have had a pyramid for a tomb. But, like Jacob, he chose to be buried in the land of my fathers, and he made his children promise to "carry up my bones from hence."

Joseph also prophesied that some day God would lead the children of Israel back to the promised land of Canaan. So ends the great "book of beginnings," with its magnificent sweep of narrative stretching from Creation itself to the emergence of the twelve tribes of Israel, each representing the descendants of one of Jacob's twelve sons.

Up to this point in the Bible story, God has revealed Himself primarily to a few individuals and their families. Now He is ready to make a covenant with a whole people. For this He will need a great leader. In the mighty drama of the Bible, such a leader is now ready to move onstage.

His name is Moses.

From Bulrushes to Burning Bush

As long as the memory of Joseph was there to protect them—and his fame lingered long—the children of Israel prospered in the land of Goshen. The little band of seventy souls that Jacob had brought with him from Canaan became a multitude. At first the native Egyptians tolerated them, but as the Hebrews grew in strength and numbers they began to hate and oppress them. Finally under a Pharaoh who "knew not Joseph," the children of Israel found themselves virtually enslaved.

Slave-owners always fear their slaves. Alarmed by the high birthrate of his captive people, Pharaoh commanded all midwives to kill male Hebrew children as soon as they were born. When the midwives ignored this murderous order, he decreed that all such children should be thrown into the Nile— and he sent his soldiers to enforce this law.

Soon after this cruel edict was handed down, a young Hebrew mother of the tribe of Levi gave birth to a son. She already had a daughter, Miriam, and another son, Aaron. Born before the extermination order, Aaron was relatively safe. But his mother knew the king's soldiers would kill the new baby if they could find him. For three months she managed to conceal her infant son, but this became steadily more difficult and dangerous. Finally she took a basket, made it waterproof, placed the child in it, and set it among the river reeds and bulrushes at a place where the ladies of the royal court came down to bathe.

The child's mother did not dare remain close by, but she left her little girl, Miriam, to watch. Soon Pharaoh's daughter herself came down with her retinue of hand-maidens. She noticed the basket in the reeds and ordered it brought to her. When she saw the wailing child, the Bible says, she "had compassion on him." She knew it was a Hebrew baby but, defying her father's fierce order, she decided to adopt it.

At that point, little Miriam came out of

her hiding place and joined the group of women who were exclaiming over the baby. We can imagine her shyly plucking at the sleeve of the princess. Would Pharaoh's daughter like a nurse from among the Hebrew people to care for the child until it was older? Miriam knew just where to find one! With the permission of the princess, she ran and called her mother. And so the child was handed back to its own parent, who kept him until he was old enough to join the royal household.

Did all this happen simply by good luck or by chance? Hardly! That young Hebrew mother planned the whole thing. She did what most everyone would do when in a tight spot. She didn't just sit there, bewailing her fate. First, she prayed about her

situation. Then, using her good brain, she took the problem to pieces, bit by bit. Where could a male Hebrew child find protection? In his own home? No. Among other Hebrew families? No. Where, then? Why, under the shadow of the same authority that was trying to destory him!

Once that inspiration came to her, the young mother worked out every move in advance. She knew where the royal princess would come to bathe. She knew she would regard the baby as a fascinating (and forbidden) toy. She counted on the compassion that dwells in all individual hearts, no matter how harsh collective decrees or actions may be. She knew that people tend to love what they protect.

Was her plan risky? Certainly. Was it brilliant? Absolutely. No wonder the baby in the bulrushes was destined some day to become one of the world's greatest leaders. If he had brains, if he had courage, if he had faith—and later he proved he had all three in abundance—he didn't acquire them by

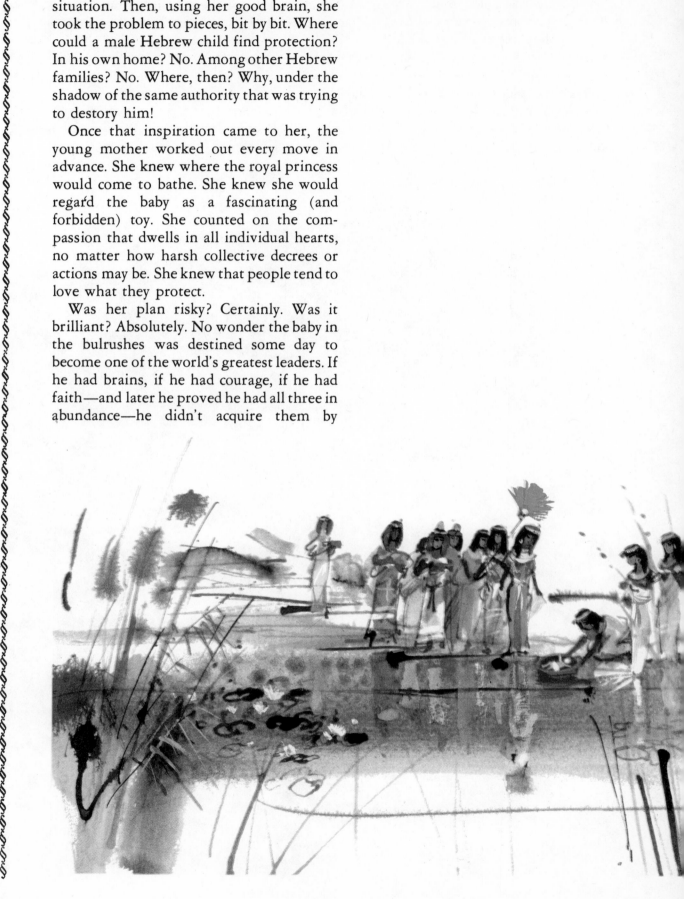

accident. He got them by inheritance from his cool-headed, courageous mother.

So Moses, as the princess named him, grew up, part Hebrew peasant and part Egyptian prince. What a combination! What a chance to observe and understand two vastly different cultures. What an opportunity to see the cruel contrasts between vast wealth and grinding poverty.

At times, no doubt, the young Moses

wondered where his deepest allegiance lay. Then one day he had a chance to find out. he came upon an Egyptian overseer beating a Hebrew slave. In a flash of fury he struck the overseer and killed him.

Now Moses was no longer a privileged member of the royal household; he was a Hebrew wanted for manslaughter. He fled far into the wilderness where Pharaoh's vengeance could not find him. In the land of Midian, deep in the southeastern part of the Sinai Peninsula, he married Zipporah, daughter of a priest, who bore him two sons. He lived as a simple shepherd, tending his father-in-law's flock. As the years passed, the life he had led in faraway Egypt began to seem like a dream.

Then one day as he was leading his flock near the slopes of Mount Horeb, also known as Sinai, he saw a remarkable thing. Not far from him a bush burst into flame. The fire burned brightly, but somehow the bush was not consumed. Astonished, Moses ventured nearer. As he did, God's voice spoke to him from the burning bush. The Lord told Moses that He had seen the suffering of the children of Israel in Egypt and had decided to rescue them. Moses was to be the Lord's instrument of deliverance. he was to go and

confront Pharaoh—a new and even harsher king was on the throne of Egypt. Then he was to lead his people to the promised land of Canaan.

Moses' first reaction was hardly one of enthusiasm. He sounded, in fact, like a negative thinker. "Who, me?" he asked the Lord incredulously. Then he began to give a host of reasons why the children of Israel would not listen to him and why the whole idea would not work.

To prove Himself to Moses, the Lord

caused two miracles to happen then and there. First Moses' shepherd's staff was changed into a serpent and back into a staff again. Next, Moses' hand was afflicted with leprosy and then instantaneously cured. Still Moses was highly dubious. He told the Lord that he was a stammerer, slow of speech, someone who could never persuade anyone to do anything.

When a man is filled with this kind of self-doubt, it's very difficult to put backbone into him. The Lord Himself had a hard time with Moses. It's interesting, though, that He chose for this great task a man who had such a low opinion of himself. It was almost as if He wanted to show mankind that one-person-plus-God can do anything. Even though Moses kept begging Him to find somebody else, the Lord would not take no for an answer. He told Moses that his brother, Aaron, would help him and that He Himself, God Almighty, would tell him what to do and say.

God also gave Moses an awe-inspiring definition of Himself. When Moses asked His name, God said to him, "I AM THAT I AM." These mysterious words can be translated in various ways: I WILL BE WHAT I WILL BE, or I AM, BECAUSE I AM. What it means is that everything else has a beginning and an end, but not God. He simply *is*, too mighty, too powerful, too infinite to be comprehended by mere men. He said to Moses, "Say unto the children of Israel, I AM hath sent me unto you." And Moses finally accepted the assignment.

The story of the burning bush can be read and understood on many levels. To the religious historian it might mark the transition from superstitious belief in fire gods or mountain spirits to an awareness of the omnipresent majesty of a single Creator. For those who respond to symbolism, it might be a way of describing how the spark of an idea can fall into a man's mind and leave him on fire with a burning desire to achieve some worthwhile goal. The mind of such a man is not consumed by the heat of his inspiration any more than the bush was consumed by the fire that enveloped it.

May we not think that every painter, every musician, every writer, every poet, or indeed anyone who creates something beautiful or something true has within him his own burning bush. The traditional word for it is *inspiration*. But when the goal is a noble one, as it was in the case of Moses, it is also the voice of God.

"Let My People Go!"

Back to Egypt came Moses, charged now with the awesome responsibility of freeing a captive people from a ruthless tyrant. His task was all the harder because the people's spirit had almost been broken by an iron dictatorship based on force and cruelty. But the fire that he had seen in the burning bush was now blazing in the mind and heart of Moses, and he was no longer hesitant and afraid.

With Aaron at his side, he sought an audience with the sneering ruler of all Egypt. He told the king that the God of the children of Israel wanted them to be given relief from their labors so that they could go into the wilderness and offer sacrifices to him.

This was a direct challenge to the royal authority, and Pharaoh was enraged. He not only refused, he ordered his slave drivers to stop supplying the chopped straw that was a necessary ingredient in the bricks of sun-dried clay that the Hebrews were forced to make. "Let them gather their own straw," said Pharaoh contemptuously. "But make sure that they meet their production quotas all the same!"

When the quotas were not met, the workers were lashed unmercifully. "Look what you've done," they cried to Moses. "You have angered the Egyptians so that they will kill us all!"

Even Moses was momentarily dismayed. "Lord," he murmured, "why did You ever send me here?"

In His reply, God repeated all His promises to Moses. And this was a God of power speaking, angry and irresistible. He said that in the end Pharaoh would be forced to give in.

Now began a dramatic struggle: centralized authority against the spirit of freedom; pagan magic against spiritual strength; the power of evil as embodied in the sadistic Pharaoh against the righteousness of a just and indignant God.

One after another, terrible plagues fell upon the Egyptians. First the life-giving waters of the Nile were turned to blood. Then, when Pharaoh remained unmoved, a horde of loathsome frogs came out of the ponds and rivers, invading people's homes, crawling into their beds, jumping into their food. To get rid of the frogs, Pharaoh agreed to let the captive people go. But when the frogs were dispersed, he went back on his word.

Then came swarms of lice and flies. Next a terrible disease struck all the domestic animals of the Egyptians, wiping out their herds. But none of these disasters fell upon the children of Israel. Sheltered by the hand of God, they were immune.

Next came boils, followed by furious hailstorms smashing trees and crops. Then clouds of locusts, so many that "they covered the whole face of the whole earth." Then a terrifying darkness fell upon the land, so thick, the Bible says, that it could be felt. Perhaps it was a terrible sandstorm; in any case, it lasted for three days, and no Egyptian could see his hand before his face.

Time and again, trying to escape from the relentless pressure, Pharaoh promised to let the captives go. But each time, once the plague was ended in response to his promise, he changed his mind.

Finally the Lord decided to send a tenth and final plague, the worst of all. In a single night, every firstborn in the land of Egypt, from the son of the great Pharaoh himself to the child of the humblest Egyptian worker, would die. Moses warned the king that this was going to happen, but "the Lord hardened Pharaoh's heart, so that he would not let the children of Israel go...."

On this dreadful night, Moses ordered each Hebrew family to kill a sacrificial lamb, take some of the blood, and mark the doorways of their homes, so that when the Angel of Death swept over the land he would see the blood and pass over the marked houses, leaving the occupants unharmed.

All took place just as Moses had predicted. When the sun rose, a great cry of anguish went up all over Egypt, for "there was not a house where there was not one dead."

Now at last word came down to Moses from Pharaoh: "Rise up... go... take your flocks and your herds... and be gone!" Knowing that this evil king might change his mind again, the children of Israel left in such a hurry that there was no time even to bake their daily bread. They wrapped the unleavened dough in pieces of cloth and took it with them. Most experts think that this critical date in Jewish history occurred in the thirteenth century before Christ. To this day, more than three thousand years later, the descendants of the people who took part in the great Exodus from Egypt eat unleavened bread in their observance of Passover.

Driving their herds before them, the refugees traveled as fast as they could. The Bible says that the Lord went before them in a pillar of cloud by day and a pillar of fire by night. Led by these mighty symbols of divine protection, sustained by faith and hope, the fugitives hurried on. But not fast enough. The tenacity of evil is unbelievable. Behind them in Egypt, the wicked Pharaoh decided that he had made a mistake in letting this supply of free labor get away. He "took six hundred chosen chariots," and the rest of his army, and led them in furious pursuit.

The children of Israel were encamped by the sea. The traditional translation calls it the Red Sea, but the original Hebrew means literally "sea of reeds." Scholars differ as to where this place was. Perhaps it was along the marshy Mediterranean coast where tides might vary enormously in different wind or weather conditions. Perhaps it was around the shores of Lake Timsah.

In any case, looking back, the children of Israel saw the dust boiling up from the racing wheels of the Egyptian war chariots, and they became panic-stricken. "Look," they screamed wildly to Moses, "here comes Pharaoh with his whole army. We are lost! We are done for! It would have been better to stay in Egypt as slaves than die here in the wilderness like dogs!"

Better slave than slaughtered. In our time, the phrase is better Red than dead. Strange how the language of cowardice repeats itself on the pages of history.

But Moses stood up and spoke to them in a voice like a great trumpet: "Stand firm! Fear not! The Lord will fight for you!"

What had happened to this eighty-year-old man who had been so weak, so vacillating, so unsure of himself? He had been touched by the finger of God, and it had changed him by changing his patterns of thought. Instead of thinking small, he had learned to think big. Instead of thinking failure, he had learned to think success. Instead of holding in his mind thoughts of doubt and weakness, he began to hold thoughts of confidence and strength. As soon as his *attitudes* changed, he began to live up to the greatness that was in him all along.

If only more of us could grasp this concept that changed thinking means changed lives! Try asking yourself this question right now: am I living up to my littlest self or to my greatest self? When you face up to that question, you're really dealing with fundamentals!

Some people are good, but only in a negative way. They don't steal, or drink too much, or take drugs. They don't run off with someone else's wife. They're good people,

but they're small people, held back by little concepts, little ambitions, little objectives.

But the story of Moses tells us that no one has to stay small. If you let yourself be touched by the finger of God, you can be much bigger than you are, more successful, happier, healthier, stronger and better in every way. That is what happened to Moses. That is why, in the face of almost certain disaster, he could cry out to the children of Israel with blazing faith and confidence, "Stand still, and see the salvation of the Lord!"

Then, says the Bible in a majestic and awe-inspiring passage, "Moses stretched out his hand over the sea; and the Lord caused the

sea to go back by a strong east wind all that night, and made the sea dry land, and the waters were divided. And the children of Israel went into the midst of the sea upon the dry ground: and the waters were a wall unto them on their right hand, and on their left."

After them came the on-rushing Egyptians, howling like wolves, their horses covered with dust and sweat, the wheels of their chariots dragging in the damp sand. Then abruptly the tide turned and the wind

blew "and the sea returned to his strength." Back came the surging waters, slowly at first, then faster, finally in an irresistible torrent that poured over the struggling army, upseting chariots, drowning horses, sweeping away whole regiments. Maddened soldiers clawed at one another as their heavy armor dragged them down. Screams and curses filled the air, then gradually died away. "Thus the Lord saved Israel that day out of the hand of the Egyptians; and Israel saw the

Egyptians dead upon the sea shore."

What a fantastic climax to an amazing story! It's one we all should remember when life's troubles seem to pursue us like avenging armies. "Stand firm!" said Moses. "Fear not!" That call to courage was magnificent thirty centuries ago. It's still magnificent today.

Forty Years of Wandering

For a little while after their miraculous deliverance from Pharaoh's army, the children of Israel were full of enthusiasm. They danced and sang and made up hymns of praise and gratitude. Then they 'resumed their march, but it wasn't long before they began to grumble about the hardships of life in the desert. Probably there were a handful of malcontents who infected the rest. "What are you doing to us?" these heart-sinkers said to Moses and Aaron. "In Egypt we may have been slaves, but at least we had meat and bread to eat. Now you have brought us out here to starve to death!"

The Lord responded to these complaints by sending flights of quail—a bird well known in that area to this day—and also a strange white substance that lay upon the ground and tasted "like wafers made with honey." Perhaps it was a sweet, sticky sap given off by certain desert shrubs—notably the tamarisk—at certain times of year. Whatever it was, the refugees were glad to get this "bread of God." They called it "manna," a word that may come from a Hebrew phrase meaning "what is it?" Exactly what it was, no one knows, but ever since, people have used the phrase "manna in the wilderness" to describe some welcome and unexpected blessing.

The quail and the manna solved the food problem, but finding water was a never-ending struggle. Plodding along, day after day, the people grew more and more sullen and discontented. They complained so constantly that Moses finally cried out in exasperation and fury, "What shall I do unto this people? They be almost ready to stone me!"

Again the Lord heard and again He miraculously intervened. He ordered Moses to strike a rock with his staff. When he did, a torrent of water gushed out, enough for the parched travelers and their thirst-maddened animals. This episode has always had strong appeal for painters. I'm told that in the catacomb paintings of the early Christians, this scene appears more often than any other in the Old Testament.

Hunger and thirst were not the only enemies that harassed the weary marchers. Their route took them across the territory of a fierce tribe of desert warriors, the Amalekites, who were descendants of Esau. Perhaps the Amalekites started the trouble with hit-and-run raids on the Israelites. Or perhaps they saw them as invaders with whom they were unwilling to share water and pastureland. In any case, it became clear to Moses that he was going to have to fight his way through.

He called upon one of the boldest and strongest of his young men, a natural-born leader named Joshua. He ordered him to handpick a group of fighting men. "Go out, fight with Amalek," Moses said. "Tomorrow I will stand on the top of the hill with the rod of God in mine hand."

As long as Moses stood there outlined against the sky with his hands raised up to heaven, the Israelites fought well. But whenever he grew weary and lowered his arms, the tide of battle turned in favor of the enemy. Finally Aaron and a man named Hur (tradition has it that Hur was the husband of Miriam, Moses' sister) stood on either side of Moses and supported his arms, holding them extended until the sun went down. Does this vivid scene foreshadow the great symbol that will dominate the New Testament—the symbol of the cross? Some people think so. In any case, Joshua and his men mowed down the Amalekites. The way across their territory was open. The great migration continued.

In the third month after they had escaped from Egypt, the children of Israel came to the wilderness of Sinai where God had first spoken to Moses out of the burning bush. And it was on the same sacred mountain that one of the great landmark events of human history now took place: the handing down of the Ten Commandments.

The drama begins like the prologue of a great play with the Lord calling to Moses from the heights of the mountain. First He reminds the children of Israel of the great things He has done for them. "Ye have seen what I did unto the Egyptians, and how I bare you on eagles' wings, and brought you unto myself." He renews His great promise to them: "If ye will obey my voice indeed, and keep my covenant, then ye shall be a peculiar treasure unto me above all people."

How amazing all this is! Man is not seeking God so much as God is seeking man. Man can't begin to reach up to the heights where God dwells, so God decides to come down to him. The children of Israel were told to get ready, because on the third day the Lord would descend in person to the top of Mount Sinai. Everyone would then know that it was God Himself, not merely the voice of Moses or any other prophet, that was speaking to them.

Sure enough, on the third day the mountain was veiled in smoke. The ground quaked. Lightning flashed, thunder roared. The whole mountain seemed to be on fire. No one could see the face of God, but in a sound like a thousand trumpets He spoke the majestic words that changed forever the moral climate of the world, beginning with the tremendous announcement of His own identity: "I am the Lord thy God...."

Given in smoke and fire on Mount Sinai, the Ten Commandments have come thundering down the centuries. Other creeds, other statements of the law have been made, have lasted a few generations, have passed away. But the Commandments remain, towering above all manmade laws and statutes. In the briefest possible form, they might be summarized as follows:

1. *One God only*
2. *No false idols*
3. *No blasphemy*
4. *The Sabbath to be kept holy*
5. *Parents to be honored*
6. *No killing*
7. *No adultery*
8. *No stealing*
9. *No lying under oath*
10. *No evil thoughts*

Scholars have pointed out that some of these principles were already recognized in the codes developed by primitive peoples. But this was the first time that the best and most important were singled out and given the direct sanction of Almighty God.

To a remarkable extent, the Ten Commandments cover man's chief obligations to his Maker and to his fellowman. The last five, in particular, are designed to safeguard the cornerstones of civilization. The prohibition against killing was essential if the community of Israel was to survive—and is essential for the same reason in every community to this day. The prohibition against adultery protects the family, the basic unit of any society. The prohibition against stealing proclaims the sacredness of property; without this concept, man will not work, and without work nothing worthwhile can be accomplished.

The prohibition against false witness— lying under oath—protects the judicial system, without which there can be no justice, no law, no order, only barbarism and chaos. Finally the tenth commandment, which is the most inclusive, recognizes that every evil action begins with an evil thought. Here the prohibition is not so much against a specific deed as against a state of mind.

Called up to the top of the mountain, shrouded in smoke and flame, Moses received the Ten Commandments written by God's own finger on tablets of stone. In God's presence, time ceased to exist for Moses. But down below where the people waited, forty days went by. The longer they waited, the more uneasy they grew. They were still a superstitious, volatile, impatient, easily discouraged group of men and women. They had undergone great hardships. They had suffered many narrow escapes. Their nerves, you might say, were not in the best possible condition. Their leader, apparently, had vanished. Who could say what had happened to him? Perhaps he had been destroyed by the lightning or the fire on the mountain. Perhaps this rather terrifying God had decided to forget all about them. In that case, they had better find another leader and another god, and they had better do it quickly.

Stirred up by the doubters and the rabble-rousers, the people came running to Aaron in a belligerent mob. After all, he had been second-in-command. "Look," they said to

him, "we don't know what's become of your brother. Here we are with no one to lead us, no one to make plans, no protection at all. You had better get busy and make us a new god, one that we can see and touch and understand, one that will lead us away from this awful mountain. Who wants to stay around here with all these storms and earthquakes? Get busy and get us out!"

Aaron's response was the typical reaction of a man who means well but is basically weak. He gave the mob the answer they wanted. Perhaps he rationalized what he was doing. Perhaps he told himself that he was just buying time until Moses returned. Perhaps he told himself that these primitive people really needed some kind of visible, tangible object to worship. "Bring me all your golden ornaments," he told them. When they did, he melted them down and fashioned a golden calf. He built an altar for it and proclaimed a feast of dedication. The

people came and offered sacrifices to the golden calf. The Bible says that they "sat down to eat and to drink, and rose up to play." They were relieved to have a god that made no demands on them. They thought that the God of Moses had forgotten them.

But the Lord had not forgotten. High on His mountain, He knew everything that happened, and He grew very angry at this backsliding of the children of Israel. Speaking to Moses, He no longer called them "my people"; it was "thy people" who had "corrupted themselves." God knew Moses well enough to know that he would plead even for this disobedient and ungrateful rabble. "Let me alone," said God (almost as if Moses could really hinder Him), "that my wrath may wax hot against them, and that I may consume them!" This is a fierce and jealous God speaking; he demands complete loyalty, nothing less, and the penalty for disobedience is death.

In His anger, God even told Moses that if He destroyed the children of Israel He would make a great nation out of Moses' own descendants. Moses must have been tempted to keep quiet and step aside, but he didn't do this. Instead, he argued fiercely and passionately with God, reminding Him of all the promises He had made to Abraham, Isaac, and Jacob. Finally—and reluctantly—the Lord agreed to spare this "stiffnecked people."

Carrying the stone tablets engraved with the new commandments, Moses went down the mountain to where Joshua was waiting for him. Together they made their way to the camp where the people were singing and dancing around the golden calf. Moses already knew what they were about, but when he saw them doing it his rage and shame boiled over. He hurled the stone tablets to the ground and smashed them, thus symbolizing the breaking of the covenant between God and the children of Israel. He took the golden calf, burnt it in the fire, and ground it to powder. He mixed the powder with water and made the people drink it as a sign of their guilt. Much of his anger was focused on Aaron. "What have you done?" he cried. "How could you bring such a great sin upon the people?"

A weak man always offers weak excuses. "You know how these people are," Aaron said, "when they get the wrong ideas in their heads. All I did was melt down some gold ornaments they gave me and—would you believe it?—out of the furnace came this wretched calf!"

That excuse wasn't good enough; Moses knew that the people had to choose between God and paganism once and for all. He hurled forth a ringing challenge: "Who is on the Lord's side? Let him come unto me!" Many of the faithful who were actually ashamed of themselves joined with Moses, but there were some who held back. In a brief, bloody interlude, all the doubters and the backsliders were killed.

Back once more to the sacred mountain went Moses, this time to make atonement for the sinners. If God would not forgive them, Moses said, he hoped the Lord would take his own life away. Angry though He was, the Lord agreed not to take vengeance on those who had promised to be "on the Lord's side." He told Moses to cut new tablets of stone, on which He would again write the Ten Commandments. He had given Moses many other lesser laws and had ordered him to build an ark, or chest, in which to keep the stone tablets. He also had given detailed instructions for building the tabernacle that would contain the ark. The Lord now promised to hover over the tabernacle in a cloud, and this cloud would guide the children of Israel in the way they should go.

When Moses finally came down from the mountain, his face shone so brightly from being in the presence of God that his followers were afraid. He had to put a veil over it until the glory faded.

The cloud led the Israelites to a place called Kadesh, close to the southern border of Canaan. "Send scouts ahead," the Lord said to Moses. "Choose one leader from each of the twelve tribes and let them spy out the country that lies ahead of you." Among the men Moses selected was the battle-tested Joshua, a member of the tribe of Ephraim. As second-in-command he chose a strong young warrior named Caleb, of the tribe of Judah.

For forty days the little band of scouts made their way carefully through the land. They found rich farmlands, vineyards heavy with grapes, fig trees, and pomegranates. Fat sheep and cattle grazed in the lush meadows. There were 'prosperous villages and strong walled cities. The people who lived in them seemed powerful and self-assured. It was clear that they would not willingly relinquish their homeland to a horde of half-starved nomads from the badlands to the south.

All this Joshua reported to Moses on his return. Caleb, the fierce young man of action, was all for invading Canaan forthwith. He was sure the children of Israel could sweep aside any opposition because the Lord would be with them.

But the other scouts were not so much men of action as men of doubt. They may have been jealous of Joshua and Caleb. Or they may simply have been timid. Anyway, they told Moses that the towns were strongly fortified, that the inhabitants were fierce and warlike. "Why," they said, "some of them were giants...so big that they made us feel like grasshoppers. Caleb must be out of his mind if he thinks we are capable of defeating people like that!"

Nothing is more contagious than fear. The more the scouts talked, the more they exaggerated, and the more they exaggerated, the more frightened their listeners became. Moses, Joshua, and Caleb were not afraid, but panic seized their followers. "These madmen will lead us to our doom," they cried. "Let's choose another leader and go back to Egypt!"

This time the Lord grew really angry with these faithless and spineless people. He caused a glowing light to appear and He spoke from it, threatening them with a plague, vowing to disinherit them altogether. Again Moses interceded, and again the Lord relented. But He was not altogether placated. He told the children of Israel that because of their doubts and lack of faith they would have to spend another forty years wandering in the wilderness. No one above the age of twenty who had murmured against God would enter the promised land. Only Joshua and Caleb would be allowed to do so. The message here seems very plain: the more a person gives in to doubt, the longer he will have to wait for the rewards of faith. And if he gives in to doubt completely, he may never taste those rewards at all.

So for forty long years the children of Israel continued to live as nomads, fed with manna, waiting for the promised day to come. Perhaps during these years they made probing attacks on the frontiers of Canaan; ancient clay tablets have been unearthed written by the Canaanites of this period to Egyptian pharaohs complaining of an invading people called the Habiru—a word fairly close to Hebrew—who seemed bent on conquering the land. Moses continued to lead, but now he was very old. Finally the Lord told him to go up to the top of Mount Nebo in the land of Moab, not far from the city of Jericho. From there he would be able to see the promised land with all its fertility and beauty, even though he himself would never set foot there.

Painfully and slowly, supported by Joshua, the old man made his way up the mountain. He was now a hundred and twenty years old, but the Bible says "his eye was not dim." He looked longingly at the goal he had struggled so hard to win. Then he died and was buried in the land of Moab, "but no man knows the place of his burial to this day."

So ended the life of the great law-giver, the mightiest of all the Old Testament prophets. Other great men would rise up to lead Israel in the years that lay ahead—Joshua would be the next. But never again would there be one like Moses, the peasant-prince whom "the Lord knew face to face."

Joshua- Sword of Israel

Between the strongly fortified city of Jericho and the desert-hardened legions of the children of Israel lay the river Jordan. It was more than just a physical barrier, it was a symbolic dividing line between two completely different religious viewpoints. The Canaanites worshiped the idol Baal and other pagan gods. Their rituals called for human sacrifice, sexual orgies, and the practice of magic. The religion of Israel forbade all these things. From their monotheism and from their special relationship with God came the tremendous drive and assurance that the children of Israel would need to conquer the rich territories that lay before them.

This is an important thing to keep in mind: the Israelites were not motivated primarily by greed. They felt that by their immoralities and their paganism the Canaanites had forfeited their right to the land. They believed that it was their own divine mission to drive them out and establish a society based on love of justice and the worship of the one true God. At the bottom of all success lies strong motivation. The Israelites believed that they were right and their enemies were wrong—and when a person or a whole people believes that, nothing can stop them.

All this is clearly indicated at the beginning of the Book of Joshua. Three times in the first ten verses the Lord urges His people to "be strong and of a good courage." He exhorts them to "be not afraid, neither be thou dismayed." Why not, in the face of such powerful enemies? Because "the Lord thy God is with thee withersoever thou goest."

Jericho is one of the oldest cities in the world, perhaps the oldest. Some scholars think people were living there eight thousand years ago. At this point in its long history it was a fortress with frowning walls and massive gates that were always closed at sundown. It was provisioned to resist prolonged seige. By any standards, it was a tough nut to crack.

As an experienced military commander, Joshua wanted to determine what preparations for defense the garrison was making, so he sent two of his men to slip into the town and bring back a report. The account of the adventures of these two spies is one of those brilliant bits of reporting that make the Bible so fascinating—the details are as vivid and convincing now as when they were first set down centuries ago.

Posing as harmless travelers, the two Israelites spent the day noting the military strengths and weaknesses of the town. When night fell, they found lodging at the home of a woman named Rahab, a harlot. Perhaps they chose her house because they knew she would not be too inquisitive about strangers. But the king of Jericho had counterespionage agents who were not asleep. They brought him word of suspicious strangers in Rahab's house. Within minutes, soldiers were at her door.

Rahab's morals left much to be desired,

93

but she was a shrewd and observant woman. She knew that the inhabitants of Jericho were terrified of the Israelites. She wanted to be on the winning side. So she hid the strangers under some flax that she was drying on her roof, and the soldiers did not find them. Her house was built on top of the city wall. Late that night when the city was dark and quiet, Rahab lowered a rope from her window to the ground outside the city. She told spies that they could escape by sliding down the rope. All she asked in return was that in the coming attack on Jericho she and her family be spared. A typical Canaanite, this Rahab: she was ready to betray a whole city full of her countrymen if by so doing she could save her own skin.

The spies were willing to make the bargain. If Rahab would display a scarlet cord in the same window when the Israelites attacked, orders would be given to spare that house and everyone in it.

So the spies came back with their report of bad morale among the defenders of Jericho. Even so, the walls were strong and the Israelites had no weapons capable of battering them down. Also there was the river to be crossed—no easy matter for the forty thousand fighting men in Joshua's army. Some leaders might have been discouraged, but Joshua had no doubts at all. The Lord had said He would be with His people; that was

all that mattered.

First the Lord took care of the river-crossing problem. It was springtime, the river was in flood, there were no bridges. But the Lord stopped the waters from flowing. He caused an earthquake, which in turn was probably followed by a landslide that blocked the river channel upstream. Such a phenomenon has been known to happen in the Jordan valley even in modern times. So the Israeli fighting men and the Ark of the Covenant and all the people were able to walk across a dry riverbed. The Bible says the people "hasted and passed over"—evidently they knew the riverbed would not stay dry for long.

From their frowning walls the defenders of Jericho must have watched with growing dread as the children of Israel carried out Joshua's instructions. For six days they marched around the city once a day with the Ark of the Covenant preceded by seven priests blowing on seven trumpets made of rams' horns. The soldiers marched in silence; no man spoke a word. It must have been hot—Jericho is some eight hundred feet below sea level—and dusty. Some of the marchers must have wondered if they were taking part in an exercise in futility.

To the citizens of Jericho this strange series of maneuvers must have been even more ominous and terrifying than the assault they were expecting. The wailing of the trumpets must have had a demoralizing effect. they must have felt that the God of these strange people, the Power that had dammed the river and made this invasion possible, was preparing some awful and supernatural fate for them.

And they were right. On the seventh day the Israelite army marched around the city not once, but seven times. On the seventh circuit, when the trumpets blew, Joshua cried out to the people, "Shout; for the Lord hath given you the city!"

There was an electrifying moment of silence. Then a great roar of voices went up. All the people shouted, all the trumpets blew, and—almost as if they were made of crystal that could be shattered by sound waves—the huge walls began to crack. Enormous chunks of masonry fell from the battlements. Great fissures appeared. The ground beneath the foundations seemed to heave and writhe. With a grinding crash of pulverized stones, the walls fell down flat, carrying with them the best fighting men of the king of Jericho.

Straight into the dust and confusion charged the Israelites, each man with sword or spear in hand. There was almost no opposition; the earthquake had completely stunned the defenders. The town was set on fire. Every living soul in the city, except for Rahab and her family, was put to the sword.

Archaeology confirms the destruction of Jericho at this time and in this manner. Actually the diggers tell us that there was a double wall around the town, and that it did indeed fall down flat. The outer wall went tumbling down a hill. The inner wall fell into the space between the two walls. Then a great fire raged, utterly wiping out the place. It was centuries before Jericho was rebuilt.

The battle of Jericho was only the first in a series of smashing victories won by Joshua. The only setbacks came when, through foolishness or willfulness, the people disobeyed the commandments of God. As long as they were faithful to the covenant in which they had promised obedience in exchange for protection, so was He.

On one famous occasion a league of five Canaanite kings fought furiously against Joshua and his men. It became apparent to the Hebrew commander that the Israelites could win a great victory only if they had more time. So Joshua commanded the sun to stand still in the heavens, and it "hasted not to go down about a whole day. And there was no day like that before it or after it, that the Lord hearkened unto the voice of a man."

The account of this ancient miracle has long troubled literalists who point out that the sun does not really move across the sky. It is the earth, they say, that turns, and if it stopped turning suddenly, centrifugal force would fling everything movable into space. But I don't see myself why the Lord might not have simply altered men's perception of time or duration on that occasion. Certainly time is a very subjective thing—five minutes in the dentist's chair can sometimes seem to me like five hours! If the Lord wanted that day to seem long, I'm sure He could have made it seem so—and I'm also sure it seemed very long to the defeated Canaanite kings and their fleeing warriors.

So the Promised Land was conquered and divided among the tribes of Israel. The Canaanites were not exterminated. They continued to live alongside the invaders in some places, and they continued their practice of pagan rites. This was a source of constant worry to Jewish leaders. At the end of his days, Joshua warned his followers not to be seduced into the worship of false gods. "Choose you this day," said Joshua, "whom ye will serve." And the people answered, "We will serve the Lord."

This exhortation of Joshua's is one that all of us might ponder from time to time. It implies that each of us has the power—here it is again, this gift of free will—to decide what comes first in our lives. It also implies that it is very easy to drift into worshiping false gods. Not idols or graven images like Baal or Astarte, but false gods nevertheless. Some men worship money. Some worship power. Some women worship personal appearance. Some bow down to social position. Some human beings are blind devotees of drink, or gambling, or sexual promiscuity.

Because there are so many false gods, Joshua's words are as challenging now as they were then. *Choose you this day whom ye will serve.* The only master truly worth serving is the Master of the Universe.

One Man Plus God Equals an Army

The years that followed Joshua's triumphs were uneasy ones for the children of Israel. The tribes were not united; at times they quarreled with one another. In some parts of Canaan their foothold was precarious; now and then the pagans were able to regain control. When this happened, the Jews attributed their misfortunes to their failure to obey God's commandments and waited hopefully for the Lord to raise up a champion to set them free.

Such was the case when a tribe known as the Midianites "came as grasshoppers for multitude" and ravaged the land so severely that they "left no sustenance for Israel, neither sheep, nor ox, nor ass."

At this point an angel of the Lord appeared to a young Israelite named Gideon and gave him a gracious greeting: "The Lord is with thee, thou mighty man of valor." Now this Gideon was a realist. He didn't consider himself a mighty man at all. Besides, he asked a bit sourly, how could the Lord be with the children of Israel when things were in such a mess? Obviously, the Lord had abandoned them to the Midianites. No, said the angel, the time had come for Israel to be liberated—and Gideon was the man who was going to do it.

Like Moses, Gideon at first was a very reluctant hero. When the Lord ordered him to destroy an altar to Baal that his father had built, Gideon did so at night because he was afraid to risk being seen in daylight. When the Lord ordered him to raise an army of liberation, fighting men flocked to his standard, but even then Gideon was afraid to tackle the Midianites. He wanted additional proof of divine support.

Testing the Lord, he put a fleece of wool on the ground and asked that the morning dew fall on it but not on the surrounding earth. When the Lord complied, he still wasn't convinced. He asked that the next night the dew fall on the ground but not on the fleece. Patiently, the Lord again complied.

By now thirty-two thousand fighting men were in Gideon's army, but this time the Lord decided to do a little testing Himself. He told Gideon that He wanted a smaller fighting force so that when victory was won it would be unmistakably the Lord's.

Gideon told his army that anyone who felt uncertain or afraid could go home. Twenty-two thousand fainthearted warriors promptly left. Ten thousand remained, but again the Lord said that number had to be reduced, and He devised another test. The details are not altogether clear, but evidently the test was to determine the combat-readiness of each soldier. When the army went down to the river to drink, most of the men laid aside their weapons, knelt down, and drank. For the moment, they were defenseless. But three hundred wary warriors scooped up water with one hand, keeping their swords in the other. Gideon kept these men and sent the others home.

Gideon's courage was growing, as it will grow in anyone who decides to stop doubting and trust the Lord. He divided his three hundred men into three companies and prepared a night attack. To each man he gave a trumpet and a deep pitcher with a lamp concealed in it. Stealthily and in total darkness they surrounded the Midianite camp. Then at a signal each man smashed his pitcher, letting the light blaze up. Each man blew a shrill blast on his trumpet. Each man shouted the agreed-upon war cry: "The sword of the Lord, and of Gideon!"

The sleeping Midianites were convinced that an overwhelming force was upon them. They fled in wild confusion, cutting one another down in their panic. "Thus was Midian subdued before the children of Israel, so that they lifted up their heads no more."

The grateful Israelites wanted to make Gideon their king, but he refused, saying that only the Lord should rule over them. Perhaps, also, he was too busy being a father to be a king—the Bible says he sired ninety sons "for he had many wives." In any case, as a result of his courage and military genius, "the country was in quietness forty years."

The message of this ancient story is clear: a host of enemies who worship false gods is nothing to be afraid of; in the last analysis they will defeat themselves. On the contrary, one man who allies himself firmly with God is the equivalent of an army.

The spirit of Gideon lives on in the famous Gideon Society, which since 1899 has distributed Bibles to countless people all over the world. It lives, too, in the hearts of any determined little band anywhere that refuses to be discouraged by what seem like hopeless odds and fights on to victory aided by "the sword of the Lord, and of Gideon."

Samson— the Hebrew Hercules

The essence of tragedy, according to the ancient Greek dramatists, is the downfall of a great man brought low by a single character defect. But the Greeks were not the first to grasp this idea. Long before Sophocles, long before Euripides, Hebrew narrators were telling a classic story of that kind—the story of Samson and Delilah.

At about the time that Gideon was subduing the Midianites, a new menace was arising to threaten the children of Israel. A powerful and warlike people called the Philistines had settled near the seacoast, occupying such towns as Gath, Ashkelon and Gaza. It is thought that they may originally have been Aegeans who were driven from their homes during the Trojan Wars. Wherever they came from, they were a dynamic and intelligent people, in some ways more advanced than the Israelites. They were skilled in the use of iron, a harder metal than the bronze that the Hebrews were accustomed to. This gave them a distinct advantage in warfare. They were also a seafaring people; one of their chief gods, Dagon, was a fishlike idol. Sometimes they fought with the Israelites, and quite often, in the days before the tribes of Israel were united under a king, the Philistines won.

During a period when the Philistines were dominant, a child named Samson was born to a member of the tribe of Dan and his wife. From birth he was a Nazarite, that is, a man dedicated to God. Such men allowed their hair to grow long as a sign of their covenant with the Lord; they never cut it. Neither did they ever taste wine or strong drink.

Samson grew up to be a young man of prodigious strength. There were stories of how he killed a lion with his bare hands, "rent him as he would have rent a kid." It was obvious that Samson was destined for great things, but he had one weakness: he liked pretty women, and particularly pretty Philistine women.

Their son's interest in pagan women troubled his pious parents. They tried to discourage him, but in vain. He insisted on marrying a Philistine girl...and walked straight into trouble. The girl's friends and relatives did not like this gigantic young Hebrew with the flowing hair and the bulging muscles. They tricked and teased him until he lost his temper and killed thirty of them. From then on it was open warfare between Samson and the fierce sea-people.

When Samson's anger was aroused, he was a dangerous antagonist indeed. On one occasion he caught three hundred foxes, tied them in pairs, tail to tail, attached flaming torches to them, and let them run through the fields and vineyards of the Philistines, destroying their crops. In retaliation, his enemies killed his wife and her family. On another occasion, when the Philistines came to arrest him, he picked up the jawbone of an ass that was lying on the ground and slaughtered them like sheep. On yet another occasion, when they thought they had him trapped inside the walled city of Gaza, he tore up the huge gates, gateposts, bars, and all, "and carried them up to the top of a hill that is before Hebron."

But Samson's great strength was no defense against the soft arms of a woman. The name of the woman was Delilah, and the Bible says that Samson loved her. The Philistines knew that he visited her often, and so they offered Delilah eleven hundred pieces of silver if she would wheedle from Samson the secret of his super-human strength. No doubt they also appealed to her patriotism, reminding her that this man was

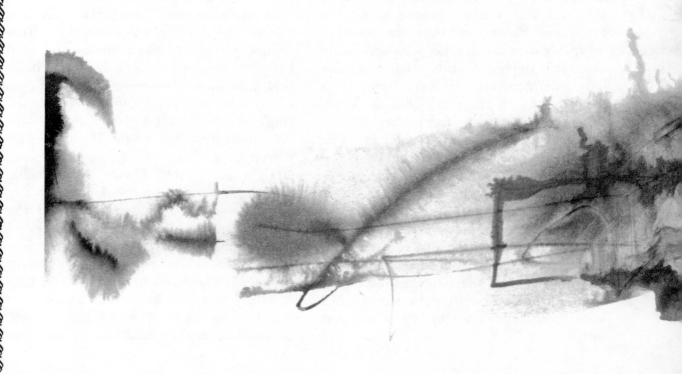

an enemy of her people. So she agreed to betray this handsome Hebrew who loved her.

At first Samson teased her by giving false clues as to the secret of his strength. First he said that if he were tied with seven bowstrings he would be helpless. She bound him, but he broke them easily. Next he said that if she used new ropes, he would be as weak as any other man. She tried that too, and he broke them like threads. The third time he told her that if she wove his hair into

a piece of cloth that she had on her loom he would be her prisoner. But when she did this, he laughed and shook himself free.

By now any normally intelligent man would have guessed that his mistress did not have his best interests at heart—and perhaps Samson did know it. But a man in love is capable of almost any madness. When Delilah wept and reproached him for making fun of her, when she scolded and complained "so that his soul was vexed unto death," he finally gave in and told her the truth—that his strength lay in his long, glossy hair.

That hair, remember, was the symbol of his dedication to the one true God. Every Hebrew listening to this story as it was told in marketplaces or around campfires knew what the hidden message really was. Samson, the hero of Israel, had turned to Delilah, the seductive symbol of paganism. If Israel turned away from the Lord, the covenant between them would be broken. In the case of Samson, the sign of that covenant was his flowing hair.

So Delilah waited until Samson slept. Then she called the Philistines out of hiding. With a razor one of them cut the seven heavy locks on Samson's head. Then they seized him. He tried to brush them aside as he always had in the past, but found he could not. They gouged out his eyes, so that he could never again be a threat to them. Then they took him to Gaza, chained him with brass chains, and put him to work turning a heavy millstone in the prison house there.

"Howbeit," says the Bible, "the hair of his head began to grow again after he was shaven." Imagine the rustle of anticipation that went around the circle of listeners when they heard that part of the story!

The Bible says nothing of the pain the blind giant must have felt, of the bitterness that must have filled his heart when he thought of Delilah, of the remorse that must have filled his spirit when he realized that just as he had turned away from God, so God had apparently turned away from him.

But not entirely. Weeks or months later the Philistines gathered together to offer a great sacrifice to Dagon, their god. The great temple was crowded with their most important leaders; the Bible says that three thousand persons were on the roof alone. They credited their god with delivering Samson into their hands, and so they decided to bring their captive out where the people could see him and jeer at him.

So the blind giant was led to a place between the great stone pillars that supported the temple. A howl of derision and hatred arose; none of the tormentors noticed that the prisoner's hair had grown long again. Samson asked the young boy who was leading him to let him lean against the two middle pillars that supported the weight of the roof. "O Lord God," he murmured, "remember me, I pray thee, and strengthen me, I pray thee." Then he encircled the two pillars with his great arms. Strength flowed back into him, and with a mighty effort he wrenched the huge stone columns from their pedestals. Down crashed the roof, the screams of the Philistines drowned out by the roar of falling masonry. Samson himself was crushed under tons of debris, but so were hundred of his tormentors. "So the dead which he slew at his death were more than they which he slew in his life."

Every culture has its folk heroes—men of marvelous strength or size: Hercules and Achilles, John Henry and Paul Bunyan. But Samson's story is deeper and truer than any of these because of its religious insights and its religious message.

"O Lord God, remember me, I pray thee, and strengthen me, I pray thee." It's a prayer that each of us might well use every morning as we go forth to meet the challenges of our own lives.

The Beloved

Without love, the world is nothing. If it were possible to sum up the teachings of Christianity in one word, that word would be love. The whole New Testament is saturated with this shining concept. But the Old Testament also has its memorable examples of the power of love to change and ennoble human lives—and one of the most memorable is the story of Ruth.

During the three hundred years when Israel was ruled by judges, before there were any Hebrew kings, a famine drove a man named Elimelech and his family from their home in Bethlehem into the country of Moab, east of the river Jordan. There his two sons married Moabite girls, although as a rule the pagan people of Moab were despised by the Hebrews. Eventually Elimelech and both his sons died. This left his widow, Naomi, and her two daughters-in-law without any men to support them. So Naomi decided to go back to Bethlehem, where she had a few relatives and where she heard the famine was ended.

She urged her two daughters-in-law, Orpah and Ruth, to stay with their own people in Moab, where it would be easier for them to remarry. Orpah (which means in Hebrew "she who turns back") agreed, but Ruth (whose name means "beloved") refused to leave her. This was not her own mother, remember; it was her dead husband's mother, and all too often there is little affection between such in-laws. But now Ruth said to Naomi in words so lovely that they ring like silver: "Whither thou goest, I will go; and where thou lodgest, I will lodge; thy people shall be my people, and thy God my God."

So Ruth and Naomi made their way back to Bethlehem, where soon they were close to starving, although in the fields around the town a fine crop of barley was being harvested. Strange to think that more than a thousand years later a Baby would be born in that same little town whose words would change the world.

Jewish law in those days permitted poor people to follow the reapers in a field, picking up stray stalks of grain, and so Ruth joined the gleaners in a field belonging to a rich man named Boaz, a distant kinsman of Naomi. Quiet and hardworking, the pretty Moabite widow attracted the attention of Boaz himself, who ordered his reapers to let extra stalks of barley fall where she could find them, and who showed her other kindnesses.

The love story develops quickly, with Naomi playing the role of matchmaker and with traditional obstacles arising that have to be overcome before boy can get girl and the happy ending be realized. Boaz decides that he wants Ruth for his wife, but custom decrees that a closer kinsman of Naomi's be given the chance to marry Ruth and raise up children to carry on the family name. Fortunately this kinsman already has a family of his own. So he declines the honor, Boaz marries Ruth, and soon—to the great joy of Naomi—they have a fine son, whom they name Obed.

It's a gentle tale, this story of Ruth, sensitively told, with a poignancy that has lasted for more than thirty centuries. The lesson would seem to be that strangers—even pagans or foreigners—can have loving hearts, and that when they do, their hearts will lead them in the right direction.

In this case, Ruth's heart led her to a true home and a true marriage and a true religion. Her son, Obed, grew up to have a son named Jesse, and he in turn became the father of a shepherd boy named David. Thus from the gentle Moabite woman came a great-grandchild destined to be Israel's greatest warrior-king, and the sweetest singer ever heard in Israel.

The Shepherd King

Not many years after Ruth the Moabitess lived and died among her adopted people, the children of Israel became convinced that if they were to survive in the Promised Land against the pressure of the Philistines and other pagan peoples they would have to be united under a king. At this time the most respected Hebrew figure was Samuel, a great prophet and man of God. Samuel pointed out a tall warrior from the tribe of Benjamin named Saul, and the people accepted him as their first king.

At first Saul proved a bold leader and courageous fighter who won some dramatic victories. But he did not always follow the word of God as laid down by Samuel. As a result, the spirit of the Lord no longer guided him. In its place came an ever-increasing melancholia punctuated by fits of violence that were close to madness.

Now the word of the Lord came to Samuel, telling him to seek out another candidate for the throne. He was told that he would find this future king among the sons of Jesse, a patriarch who lived in the little town of Bethlehem.

Jesse, grandson of Ruth and Boaz, had eight sons, the youngest a mere lad who spent most of his time on the lonely hillsides tending his father's sheep. This youngster, named David, was handsome, gifted, and brave. When Samuel saw him, he anointed the boy with the sacred oil as a sign that one day he would be king.

David himself had no such ambitions. He whiled away the long hours in the hills by playing his harp, composing songs to amuse himself, and practicing with his shepherd's sling, the weapon he used to drive off the lions and bears that preyed on the flocks. He was amazed when messengers arrived from Saul's court. The king had heard of David's great musical gifts. Music seemed to soothe the black moods that descended on him from time to time. He wanted David to come and be his harpist and live at the royal court.

By this time the children of Israel were in a state of constant warfare with the Philistines who lived on the nearby coast and made constant raids into the hill country. At one point the Philistine invaders brought with them a giant of a man, over nine feet tall, so huge and ferocious that when he challenged any of Saul's warriors to single combat, not one dared to face him.

While this monster was terrorizing the Hebrew ranks, David happened to visit three of his older brothers who were soldiers with Saul's army. The sight of Goliath strutting about and bellowing his threats infuriated him. "Who is this miserable pagan," he cried, "who thinks he can defy the armies of the living God?" He declared that he was willing to accept Goliath's challenge and meet him in hand-to-hand combat.

No one thought the rash teenager had a chance against the terrifying giant. Saul tried to persuade David to wear his royal armor, but it was too heavy and clumsy for the slender redhead. He decided to face Goliath with nothing but his shepherd's staff, his sling, and five smooth stones that he selected from a nearby brook.

Both armies stared in amazement as the youth walked calmly toward what seemed like certain death. Goliath lumbered forward brandishing his enormous spear while another Philistine soldier staggered under the weight of his huge shield. Roaring threats and curses, the giant promised to feed David to "the fowls of the air, and to the beasts of the field." In reply, David whirled his sling around his head. At exactly the right moment he released the stone with tremendous force and deadly accuracy. It struck Goliath in the forehead, stunning him. Down he crashed, like a great oak struck by lightning. Swiftly the shepherd boy ran

forward, drew the giant's own sword out of its sheath, and cut off his head. Astounded and heartened by this incredible victory, the Hebrew army plunged across the valley and routed the foe on the opposite mountainside.

Overnight David found himself a national hero. Saul gave him one of his daughters in marriage. Saul's son, Jonathan, became David's closest friend. He and David led many successful campaigns against the Philistines.

But gradually, as David's fame and popularity grew, Saul's affection for him turned to jealousy and hatred. Twice, in fits of unprovoked rage, the half-demented king hurled his javelin at the young, harpist. Finally David had to flee for his life. He became an outlaw, living in caves, harassed and hunted by Saul and his soldiers. In the end, he had to take refuge with the hated Philistines, who welcomed him as an enemy of Saul.

By this time, Saul had become a pathetic caricature of a king. He knew the Philistines were preparing a major offensive against him. He had driven his ablest soldier—David—into exile. Samuel was dead; he could not longer turn to the old prophet for advice. Frantically Saul tried to ascertain the will of the Lord, but no sign, no revelation came to him. Finally, in desperation, he decided to consult a medium, although previously he had banished all sorcerers and magicians from his realm.

Saul's servants told him about a woman living in a place called Endor who was said to be capable of summoning up the spirits of the dead. Saul went to her in disguise, by night, but she recognized him anyway. When he guaranteed her protection, she did call up an apparition that seemed to be the ghost of Samuel. But this gave little comfort to Saul. The spirit predicted that the next day the children of Israel would be defeated in battle by the Philistines. Saul and his sons, the ghost added, would be slain.

Everything the ghost of Samuel predicted came true. Jonathan and his two brothers

were killed in battle. Saul was so badly wounded by arrows that he fell on his own sword rather than be captured alive by his enemies. The defeated Hebrews were split into two monarchies. In the south, David became king of Judah. In the north, one of Saul's surviving sons became king of Israel.

Eventually this son of Saul was assassinated, and David was able to unite the two kingdoms. He captured the city of Jerusalem and made it his capital. He pushed back his enemies on all fronts until Israel became recognized as a powerful nation, not just a handful of divided tribes. All men respected and honored David. He had many wives and concubines. Everything seemed to be going well. The Lord was pleased with him. And then this great but also very human king made a grievous error. He became involved with another man's wife.

The other man was Uriah, a captain in the king's army. While Uriah was taking part in a military expedition, David remained in Jerusalem. One day from the roof of his palace he happened to see a woman bathing in the courtyard of a house nearby. It was Bathsheba, Uriah's wife. She was so beautiful that the king became infatuated. He summoned her to the palace, treated her like one of his concubines, then sent her home again.

That might have been the end of it, but shortly Bathsheba sent word to David that she was going to have a child, and that he was the father. As an all-powerful monarch, David might simply have ignored this message, but he didn't. He arranged to have Uriah ordered into the fiercest fighting. When Uriah was killed, David married Bathsheba himself.

"But," says the Bible, "the thing that David had done displeased the Lord." He sent the prophet Nathan to tell David that Bathsheba's child would die soon after it was born. Moreover, David would be punished by violence and treachery inside his own family.

David was already sorry for what he had done, and he said so publicly. But all the grim prophecies came true. Bathsheba's first child did die. A few years later David's favorite son, Absalom, led a conspiracy against his father and tried to seize the throne. David's loyal troops finally defeated the rebels, but in the battle Absalom's mule ran beneath the low-spreading branches of a great oak tree, the young prince's head was caught fast, and while he dangled there helplessly David's soldiers killed him. When the king was told that his son was dead, his grief was pitiful. The wages of sin are never easy to pay, and certainly they were not in David's case.

Altogether, David reigned for forty years.

Perhaps because he felt he owed her something, he promised Bathsheba that another child of hers, Solomon, would inherit the throne. David kept that promise. When he felt his life beginning to ebb away, he called in the young man. "Be thou strong..." he told him, "and show thyself a man, and keep the charge of the Lord thy God, to walk in his ways ... that thou mayest prosper in all that thou doest...."

Thirty centuries have passed, but David's loyalty and courage and faith in God still live on in the hearts of men. Each one of us can draw hope from the knowledge that although David was a sinner, as we are sinners, God forgave and loved him, as He forgives and loves us.

The King with the Understanding Heart

It is the tenth century before Christ. In a great hall, an oriental monarch sits on his throne, arrayed in splendid robes. The throne itself is a marvelous creation of carved ivory overlaid with gold. Around the king stand his courtiers, also richly dressed, sparkling with jewels. Light flashes on the burnished armor and weapons of the king's bodyguard. A counselor skilled in the law brings forward petitioners who have grievances, for the king is sitting in judgment—and his decisions are final.

Two women are brought forward. They prostrate themselves before the throne. They are women of a very low class—harlots in fact. Their dispute has to do with a child, a naked baby lying in a basket. It is only a few days old.

Each woman claims that the child is hers. They live in the same house and both gave birth to babies at about the same time. Then one of the babies died. Now one of these mothers is claiming that the other stole her living child and put the dead one in its place. There are no other witnesses. It is one woman's word against the other's.

The great king lowers his head and deliberates for a moment. Then his voice rings out: "Bring me a sword!"

The captain of the guard draws his glittering blade and offers it to the king. "Take the sword," says the king, "and divide the living child in two. Give half to one woman and half to the other."

There is stunned silence in the great hall. This is a barbaric age, but no one had foreseen such a verdict. The captain raises the sword above the helpless infant. "Wait!" cries one of the women, bursting into tears.

"Let her have the child. Do not kill it!" The other woman mutters, "It shall not belong to either of us. Divide it!"

The razor-sharp blade is poised above the child. But the king holds up his hand. "Stop!" he orders. "Give the living child to the first woman. She is its mother!"

With a cry of relief and gratitude, the true mother picks up her baby while the other woman slinks away. "And," says the Bible, "all Israel heard of the judgment... and they feared the king: for they saw that the wisdom of God was in him."

Where did Solomon get this wisdom, of which this story is the most famous example? He got it from the source of all wisdom: God Himself. Soon after he became king, Solomon had a dream in which the Lord appeared and said to him, "Ask what I shall give thee." Instead of asking for great wealth, or long life, or power over his enemies, Solomon humbly asked for "an understanding heart." The Lord was pleased with this request and granted it.

So Solomon, son of David, is known to this day as one of the wisest men who ever lived. Like his father, he was gifted with great literary skill. Tradition assigns The Song of Solomon to him, and the Bible says that "he spake three thousand proverbs: and his songs were a thousand and five."

People came from all over the world to see Solomon's magnificence and listen to his wisdom. One of the most glamorous visitors was the Queen of Sheba, who came with a great caravan of "camels that bear spices, and very much gold, and precious stones." She asked the world's wisest ruler some "hard questions," and he answered them all. She was amazed by the number of his chariots and horsemen. (The Bible says that he had fourteen hundred chariots and twelve thousand horsemen, figures that seemed incredible until excavations at Megiddo showed that this one site had room for 450 horses and 150 chariots.) Solomon told her about his far-reaching fleet of ships that brought him gold from Ophir (no one is quite sure where these fabulous gold mines were), and silver, and exotic cargoes of "ivory, and apes, and peacocks."

What impressed the Queen of Sheba most of all was the magnificent House of God that Solomon had built. The construction of this temple took seven years, and there was nothing like it in the ancient world. Great cedars of Lebanon (belonging to Hiram, king of Tyre) were felled and floated down the Mediterranean coast in huge rafts. Solomon paid Hiram for this durable and sweet-smelling wood by sending him vast amounts of grain and olive oil. The finest artisans and craftsmen were brought to Jerusalem. Marvelous and intricate carvings were everywhere. Even the floor was "overlaid with gold."

The Lord was pleased with the temple and consented to dwell in it, but He was less

pleased with some of Solomon's other activities, particularly his custom of including pagan princesses among his many wives. No doubt Solomon's motives were often political; he married Pharaoh's daughter, for example, in order to obtain an alliance with Egypt. Being a wise man, he believed that accommodation through diplomacy was preferable to conquest by the sword.

Nevertheless, Biblical law forbade marriage between Hebrews and the nationals of certain other countries. Even worse, once he had married these princesses (the Bible says that there were seven hundred of them, not to mention three hundred concubines), Solomon often found it expedient to let them go on worshiping their false gods. This entailed bringing in foreign priests and permitting the construction of pagan shrines of worship. The inevitable result was a dilution of the traditional monotheism of the Hebrew people.

Great material prosperity marked Solomon's reign, and new heights of magnificence and splendor. All the same, a spiritual decline from the rugged faith of David had begun. For the people, difficult days lay ahead.

Dark Days and Mighty Prophets

High on the slopes of Mount Carmel an extraordinary scene was being enacted. On a stone altar was piled wood, with a slaughtered animal ready to be offered as a burnt sacrifice. Around the altar, four hundred and fifty pagan priests were dancing, leaping, and staggering in varying degrees of religious frenzy. They were shouting prayers, pleas, and exhortations to Baal, the sky god who—so they believed—controlled the weather. A terrible three-year drought was afflicting the land. If Baal were placated, he might send rain.

But more was at stake than rain. The slopes of the mountain were covered with people watching anxiously, because this gathering was really a confrontation between two religions, a contest between the pagan priests of Baal and a lone prophet of the God of Israel named Elijah.

Ever since the death of Solomon, paganism had been making steady inroads into the faith of Israel. As that faith diminished, troubles increased. The Egyptians had invaded the land and carried off the magnificent treasures of the temple. Solomon's successors had fought among themselves until the empire built by David was hopelessly divided. Now the present king of Israel, Ahab, had taken a pagan wife, a cruel and domineering woman named Jezebel. A fanatical follower of Baal, this pagan queen was determined to make her religion prevail in the land—and Ahab was too weak to stand up to her.

Only Elijah had the courage to defy Jezebel. It was he who predicted that because of the idolatry of the people, the Lord would withhold rain. Now, in an amazing display of courage and confidence, he had challenged the priests of Baal to a contest. Let two altars be built, he said, let two burnt offerings be prepared, but no flame be touched to the wood on either altar. Then each side would attempt to call down miraculous fire from heaven to kindle the wood on the altar. "And the God that answereth by fire, let him be God!"

The priests of Baal had to accept the challenge; to refuse would be the equivalent of admitting that their sky god was inferior to Elijah's God. They prepared their altar. All day they danced around it, calling upon Baal, gashing themselves with knives (the shedding of blood on the part of the worshiper was a well-established pagan practice), whipping themselves into such frenzy that some foamed at the mouth and others fell twitching to the ground. But nothing happened. The people stared as Elijah mocked the priests, suggesting sarcastically that perhaps their god was busy talking and could not hear, or perhaps had gone on a journey somewhere.

Finally when it was clear that the incantations of the priests were futile, Elijah took twelve stones symbolizing the twelve

tribes of Israel. With the twelve stones he built a crude altar and dug a trench around it. He placed firewood and portions of a slaughtered bullock on the altar. Then to the amazement of the watching people he took four barrels of water and poured it on the altar, leaving everything soaking wet. The pouring out of water in time of drought was an old nomadic ritual; perhaps Elijah was using it to remind the people of their old desert ways of approaching the one true God as compared to the frenzied self-mutilation of the priests of Baal. Or perhaps he was determined to show that no secret spark of fire was hidden in the wood. In any case, the altar and everything on it was drenched, and the water filled the trench he had dug.

Then, while the people stared, the old man held up his hands toward heaven and prayed: "Hear me, O Lord, hear me, that this people may know that thou art the Lord God!"

Instantly, with a blinding flash, a tremendous flame came lancing out of the sky. Perhaps it was lightning. Perhaps it was something entirely supernatural; whatever it was, the Bible says that "the fire of the Lord fell." So fierce was the heat that the sacrificial animal, the wood, the stone altar—even the dust around it was utterly consumed. The water in the trench turned to steam and vanished. The priests of Baal cowered to the ground, but Elijah stood there unmoving, his arms raised to the sky. For a moment, an awe-filled silence prevailed. Then, with a shout, the people turned on the false prophets of Baal and killed them all. Almost at once, the Bible says, "the heaven was black with clouds and wind, and there was a great rain." The drought was broken, and all Israel trembled at this terrifying demonstration of the power of the one true God.

As the generations rose and fell, the Lord continued to speak to the people through a mighty succession of prophets. All preached the need for repentance, all warned of the dangers of idolatry. But again and again the spiritual integrity of the children of Israel was weakened, and wave after wave of pagan invaders rolled over them. The northern kingdom of Israel was larger and more populous than the southern kingdom of Judah, but it was also more exposed, and its fertile lands were more attractive to marauders from beyond its borders. In 720 B.C. the Assyrians swooped down and carried off the best of the people—the artisans, craftsmen, leaders, and scholars—replacing them with other captured peoples who intermarried with the remaining Israelites and became known as Samaritans, a mixed breed regarded with some hostility and contempt by pure-blooded Jews even as late as Jesus' day.

Nineteen years later, under their fierce king Sennacherib, the Assyrians rolled to the gates of Jerusalem. The prophet Isaiah predicted that they would not capture the city, and they didn't. The Bible says that the angel of the Lord slew 185,000 Assyrians (perhaps He sent the bubonic plague to decimate the pagan armies), and the city was saved.

But not for long. In 586 B.C. Nebuchadnezzar, king of Babylon, took Jerusalem, destroyed the city and Solomon's temple, and carried off the people in what became known as the Babylonian captivity. The prophet Jeremiah had predicted this national disaster: "Thus saith the Lord of hosts; Because ye have not heard my words...this whole land shall be a desolation, and an astonishment; and these nations shall serve the king of Babylon seventy years."

So it seemed that the light that Israel had brought into the world—faith in the one true God—was in danger of being extinguished altogether. But the Lord continued to send a series of extraordinary men to keep that flame alive. Limitations of space will not let us consider all of them, but no retelling of the Bible story can fail to mention two: the prophet who made a meal for a fish, and the prophet who managed not to make a meal for a den of lions.

The Most Famous Fish Story

If you asked a hundred strangers on the street to name the most famous fish story in the world, the majority would no doubt reply, "Jonah and the Whale." If you pressed them for further details, the majority of this majority would probably say that Jonah spent some time inside the whale but finally managed to emerge intact from these unusual surroundings. If you then asked them *why* Jonah was in this "great fish" (the Bible doesn't say it was a whale), you *might* get an informed answer—but then again you might not.

Which is a pity, because this little book—only four short chapters—contains a message far more important than any fish story, however famous. The message is that God does not want us to hate or despise any of our fellow human beings, even when we think we have good cause. The story of Jonah deals with bigotry. Jonah was a prophet of the Lord, but he was also a narrow-minded, stubborn, vengeful bigot.

The principal object of his hatred in the book that bears his name (his name means "dove," incidentally) was the city of Nineveh, which around the eighth century B.C. had become the capital of Assyria. The Assyrians were responsible for much suffering in Israel and were hated accordingly. Jonah was the kind of man who thinks that whatever he believes is right and whatever he does not believe is wrong. As a good Hebrew, therefore, he despised all Gentiles. But of all Gentiles, he hated the Assyrians most.

Therefore, when the word of the Lord came to Jonah telling him to go to Nineveh and turn the people away from their sins, he did not want to go. If the Assyrians were sinful—and he knew they were—that was fine. So far as he was concerned, the sooner the wrath of God descended on them, the better.

So instead of obeying the Lord, Jonah decided to run away to some place where the word of God could not reach him (a curious echo, here, of the primitive belief that the jurisdiction of a deity stopped at the borders of the country that acknowledged him). He went to the seaport town of Joppa, found a ship leaving port, paid his fare, and got aboard.

But the Lord had no intention of letting Jonah get away with this sort of disobedience. Actually, Jonah's physical flight was just a reflection of his bigotry and intolerance—which is also a flight from God. So the Lord caused a tremendous storm to arise. Howling winds and mountainous seas battered the ship until it was in danger of sinking. The sailors frantically threw cargo overboard to lighten ship, and they prayed to their pagan gods, but the situation steadily grew worse. At last, convinced that the behavior of someone on board had angered the gods, they drew lots to see who it was—and the lot fell upon Jonah.

Jonah knew perfectly well why the storm had arisen. He told the sailors that to save their lives they had better throw him overboard. They were humane men, these pagans whom Jonah despised, and at first they refused. But when hours of hard rowing got them nowhere, they were forced to take Jonah's advice. They tossed him overboard, and the storm died down.

"Now," says the Bible, "the Lord had

prepared a great fish to swallow up Jonah. And Jonah was in the belly of the fish three days and three nights."

What a mighty chorus of controversy this one verse has called forth! Skeptics say it would have been impossible for a whale (but it wasn't necessarily a whale!) to swallow a man in the first place, and certainly he could not have survived three days inside a fish. Their opponents argue that if the Lord wanted such a thing to happen, He could arrange a fish with special living quarters just as easily as He called up the storm in the first place. The symbol-seekers contend that Jonah's stay inside the fish probably represents the unhappy days when the children of Israel were carried off into Babylon and had to live as exiles in a foreign and unhappy environment far from home. Others scornfully say that the story of Jonah is just a parable anyway and that therefore it's foolish to argue about its historical truthfulness.

Be all that as it may, the Book of Jonah is a portrait of a stubborn and willful man who hated to let go of his hatred. As such it has a lot to say to a great many of us. So let's get back to the story.

Inside the great fish, Jonah prays to the Lord. His prayer is heard. The fish deposits him on dry land. But is he now cured of his bigotry? Not at all! He still hates the people of Nineveh as much as ever. He still hopes the Lord will utterly destory them—and soon.

But the Lord decides to give Jonah a second chance. Again he orders him to go to Nineveh and urge to people to mend their ways. This time Jonah doesn't dare disobey. He goes and preaches so eloquently that the Assyrians *do* repent. But this "displeased Jonah exceedingly, and he was very angry." It was bad enough to think that these miserable Assyrians might not suffer the vengeance of the Lord. To think that he, Jonah, was responsible was more than he could bear. He was so disgusted that he wanted to die. He went and sat "on the east side of the city," hoping that maybe somehow after all it would be destroyed.

It was very hot on the east side of the city, so the Lord obligingly caused a vine with broad leaves to grow up and give Jonah some shade. Then, because He was still trying to make His point with Jonah, He caused a worm to come and destroy the vine so that it withered away and left Jonah in the hot sun again. "Are you unhappy," asked the Lord, "because this vine has been destroyed?"

"Very unhappy!" said Jonah.

"Well, now," said the Lord, "you're sorry about this vine, which you didn't even plant, and which came up in one night and perished in one night. If you feel sorry for this vine, why shouldn't I take pity on Nineveh, the great city with 120,000 people who are so confused and misguided that they don't know their right hand from their left?"

The story ends right there. If Jonah had anything to say, which is doubtful, the Bible doesn't record it. But every Hebrew who heard the story—and it is still read in synagogues on the Day of Atonement—understood the message: that the love of God is not confined to any one people, and that any man who hates his fellow man is really in rebellion against his Creator.

Daniel- Prophet in Exile

During their long captivity in Babylon, many of the children of Israel were homesick and miserable. Their nation no longer existed. They wept whenever they thought of their homeland. Their magnificent temple was a heap of rubble. Some were convinced that God had turned His face away from them forever.

But Nebuchadnezzar, their fierce conqueror, did not always treat his captives badly. He had great respect for the energy and intelligence of these descendants of David and Solomon. He was determined to use these qualities to strengthen and support his own kingdom.

Therefore he decreed that the most promising young Hebrews be taught the Babylonian language and customs. Four of the brightest young men thus chosen were named Daniel, Shadrach, Meshach, and Abednego. When their education was complete, the king himself examined them personally and found that in matters of wisdom and all forms of statecraft they were ten times wiser than any of his own advisers. So he placed them all in positions of authority—a step that may have been good for the kingdom but also aroused bitter resentment and jealousy in the hearts of the king's own Babylonian subjects.

Just as his ancestor Joseph had done in Egypt so many centuries earlier, Daniel made a great impression on the king by interpreting a dream for him. None of the king's Chaldean astrologers or soothsayers could even discuss the dream, because the king could not remember it himself—he only knew that he had had a frightening nightmare. Daniel not only told the king what he had dreamed, he explained it as a prophecy of coming events. He also told the king that he, Daniel, had no supernatural powers of his own. It was the God of Israel who made such things possible.

Nebuchadnezzar was impressed, but not impressed enough to become a convert to Daniel's religion. As sometimes happens with important people, his favorite deity was himself. He caused a great golden image of himself to be set up, ninety feet tall, and decreed that everyone should bow down and worship it.

Almost everyone in Babylon hastened to obey, because the penalty for disobedience was a hideous death by fire. But, remembering the Second Commandment given to Moses, the three young Hebrews Shadrach, Meshach, and Abednego refused. Their rivals at court promptly told the king. When the angry monarch threatened them with death in the fiery furnace unless they changed their minds, the young men defied him to do his worst. "Our God whom we serve," they said, "is able to deliver us from the burning fiery furnace, and he will deliver us out of thy hand, O king!"

Nebuchadnezzar was not used to talk like that from anyone. He ordered the furnace to be heated seven times hotter than ever before. Bound with ropes and fully clothed, the three defiant Hebrews were hurled into the roaring fire while the king looked grimly on. But then, through the raging flames, Nebuchadnezzar saw an incredible sight. Instead of dying in agony, the three victims were walking around in the midst of the fire. Furthermore, it seemed to the king's unbelieving gaze that a fourth person was with them. When the king called to them, Shadrach, Meshach, and Abednego walked out unharmed. All the witnesses saw that the fire had no power over their bodies, "nor was a hair of their head singed."

Who was the fourth person in the fiery furnace? The Bible gives no definite answer; it merely says that to the amazed king his form was "like the Son of God." One tradition has it that this fourth figure was the angel Gabriel, sent by the Lord to protect His loyal followers. In any case, the Babylonian ruler was sufficiently impressed to issue a decree that anyone speaking ill of the God of Israel would be cut in pieces, "because," he said, "there is no other God that can deliver after this sort."

The message of the fiery furnace is plain enough. It is that those who have the courage of their convictions and do what is right regardless of the consequences may pass through fire, but they will also find themselves supported and protected by a power greater than themselves.

Sooner or later all of us come up against situations where doing the right thing calls for moral or physical courage. A high school youngster is challenged by his pot-smoking friends to try marijuana; in that case the fiery furnace is the fear of being considered a sissy or a square if he refuses to go along. A college sophomore may be tempted to cheat on an examination; in that case the fiery furnace is the fear of failing the course. A married couple hesitates to ask a member of a minority group to their house for fear of "what the neighbors will say." Life is full of these fiery furnaces, but courage and honesty lend their own protection to those who do not cave in and worship whatever the false idol may be.

In time the great king Nebuchadnezzar died, and his son Belshazzar ruled. He had less respect for the God of Israel than his predecessor, because when he "made a great feast to a thousand of his lords," he brought out the gold and silver vessels that had been taken from the temple in Jerusalem and let his wives and concubines drink from them while they praised his pagan gods.

At this desecration, the fingers of a man's hand apeared and wrote four words on the plaster of the wall of the king's palace: *mene, mene, tekel, upharsin.* White-plastered walls were designed to reflect the flickering light of torches and candles; excavations in Babylon had revealed such rooms. On a wall like this the writing appeared, and when the king saw it, the Bible says, "his knees smote one against another."

Frantically he summoned his astrologers and fortune-tellers. None could tell him what the ominous inscription meant. Finally the queen recalled that Daniel, one of the captive Jews, had been able to interpret Nebuchadnezzar's dream. She urged her son to have Daniel brought in, and the king sent for him.

According to Jewish tradition, the writing was in Hebrew. The Babylonians could read the letters, but they could not understand them because the message was in the form of an anagram in which the words had to be read by reading downwards. In any case, Daniel had no trouble in deciphering the supernatural writings. He told Belshazzar that it meant that the days of his kingdom were numbered, that he had been judged and found wanting, and that his nation was to be conquered by the Medes and Persians. And that very night, the Bible says, Belshazzar was slain and Darius the Mede received the kingdom.

From the start, Darius was impressed with Daniel. He made him one of the chief administrators in the land. He planned eventually to "set him over the whole realm." As a result, jealous princes and satraps of the realm sought for a way to get rid of Daniel.

The trap they devised was a clever one. They persuaded Darius to issue a decree forbidding anyone in the kingdom to make a petition to god or man other than the king himself. The penalty was spelled out: anyone who disobeyed the decree would be thrown to the lions. Once the king signed the order, it became immutable. Nothing under any circumstances was allowed to interfere with a "law of the Medes and Persians."

As the jealous satraps well knew, every

day Daniel knelt at his window facing in the direction of Jerusalem and prayed to the God of his fathers. When he continued this practice despite the king's decree, his rivals demanded that the law be put into effect and that Daniel be thrown to the lions.

When the king heard the charges, "he was sore displeased with himself, and set his heart on Daniel to deliver him: and he labored till the going down of the sun to deliver him." But he was trapped by his own decree. He said to Daniel, "Thy God, whom thou servest continually, he will deliver thee." And he cast him into the lions' den.

All night this good-hearted pagan king agonized over what he had done. He refused all entertainment, and "his sleep went from him." At daybreak he hurried to the den and cried out in "a lamentable voice," asking Daniel if his God had indeed been able to save him. Great was his relief when the prophet replied that the Lord had sent an angel to shut the lions' mouths. The prophet was taken out of the den, and in a grim gesture of revenge the king had all his accusers thrown in—"them, their children,

and their wives; and the lions had the mastery of them, and brake all their bones in pieces..."

So Daniel was restored to a place of high honor during the remainder of the reign of Darius and in that of Cyrus the Persian, who succeeded him.

Cyrus turned out to be the most magnanimous ruler of all. In the first year of his reign he issued a decree that the captive Jews be allowed to return to their homeland and rebuild the temple and Jerusalem, the City of David. They were to be allowed to take with them all the gold and silver vessels stolen from the temple by Nebuchadnezzar. With great rejoicing and high hopes, the children of Israel began the long march home. As Jeremiah had predicted, their captivity in Babylon had lasted seventy years.

Many difficulties lay ahead of them. The Samaritans who occupied the territory did not welcome the return of these determined and dedicated people. When they reached Jerusalem, they found it almost abandoned, little more than a heap of scattered stones. But they doggedly set about rebuilding the walls, and in time they rebuilt the temple also.

More than fifteen hundred years had now elapsed since Abraham left the city of Ur. In that time, the children of Israel had changed greatly; they were no longer nomads and keepers of sheep; now they were tillers of the soil, artisans, city dwellers. Their concept of their God had changed greatly, too. Through the harsh days in Egypt, through the wanderings in the wilderness, through the rise of David's kingdom, the God of Israel had often been thought of primarily as a God of war, capricious, often angry, capable of awful threats and fearful vengeance. Gradually He became less harsh and frightening, but for a long time He was still thought of as a tribal deity, the exclusive possession of the tribes of Israel, their own special God who was above all other gods and who took little or no interest in other nations or other peoples.

Slowly, painfully, man had learned to think of God as a Being of patience and justice and mercy as well as a Being of infinite power. Now another idea was struggling to be born, the idea that, all-wise and all-powerful and all-knowing though He was, the Creator of all things was primarily and eternally and above all a God of love.

So the slow centuries passed. Conquerors still came, trampling through the ancient land of Canaan. Four hundred years after the rebuilding of the temple it was the Roman invader, taking over Palestine almost casually in his relentless march toward world domination. Rome was cruel, Rome was invincible, but Rome was also practical. By and large, she did not interfere with the religion of the people she conquered. Unless that religion preached revolt or sheltered rebels against the rule of Rome, the conquering legions tended to regard it with tolerance or contempt.

With this iron heel on their necks, the children of Israel endured and waited and hoped for the Messiah to come. Their greatest prophets had promised that some day he would appear. "For unto us," Isaiah had cried, "a child is born, unto us a son is given; and the government shall be upon his shoulder: and his name shall be called Wonderful, Counsellor, The mighty God, The everlasting Father, The Prince of Peace."

In what form would this expected Deliverer come? Nobody knew. Some hoped that he would come surrounded by armies of avenging angels that would sweep the hated Romans into the sea. Others thought he might be a great king whose glory would eclipse Solomon's. The prophecies themselves seemed contradictory. Some spoke of a man of sorrows who would be scorned and rejected, others of a ruler whose kingdom would have no end.

But no one guessed the truth, which was that the Prince of Peace would appear as a tiny baby, born in a manger because there was no room at the inn.

The New Testament

The Night
the Angels Sang

The greatest story in the world begins as quietly as a single snowflake drifting down into a silent forest at midnight. It begins in the home of a young girl named Mary who lived almost two thousand years ago in the town of Nazareth in the province of Galilee.

There is much that we don't know about this extraordinary event. We don't know at what time of day or night it happened. We don't know what Mary was doing: perhaps she was sewing or weaving, perhaps she was daydreaming as young girls do, perhaps she was saying her prayers. We don't even know what Mary looked like, although ever since, the greatest artists in the world have been trying to guess.

What we do know is that at one unique instant in time, so unique that it divided every other event into "before" and "after," God sent His messenger, the angel Gabriel, to speak to Mary. "And the angel came in unto her and said, 'Hail, thou that art highly favored, the Lord is with thee...' "

What was the reaction of this gentle young girl, still in her teens no doubt, perhaps her early teens? Astonishment, certainly. Awe and a twinge of alarm perhaps...surely an angel is different in manner and appearance from mortal men.

The angel knew that she must be startled, so he tried to reassure her: "Fear not, Mary: for thou hast found favor with God." He went on to tell her that she would bear a son and name him Jesus, which means "the Lord

is salvation," or, "the Lord will save." This child, the angel said, would be called the Son of the Highest, and his kingdom would have no end.

Now the astonishment in Mary's mind became perplexity. She did not doubt the truth of the angel's words, but she knew a baby had to have a father as well as a mother. She loved a young carpenter named Joseph, but no wedding ceremony had taken place. How, then, could this thing that the angel was predicting come about? She hesitated, then put her question into words. "How," she asked timidly, "shall this be?"

The angel must have seemed to her like a towering flame as he replied. "The Holy Ghost shall come upon thee," he told her, "and the Highest shall overshadow thee." What a stupendous thing for a young girl to be told with no preparation, no warning! Only a pure and trusting heart could bear to contemplate it. But Mary had such a heart. She must have felt deep joy flood through her as she bowed her head in humble acceptance. "Behold," she murmured, "the handmaid of the Lord; be it unto me according to thy word."

This was not Gabriel's only appearance during this miraculous year. Saint Luke tells us that six months earlier the angel had also appeared to Mary's cousin Elizabeth and had predicted that she too would bear a remarkable son. Later he would be known as John the Baptist. Thus we know that John, six

months older than Jesus, was also his kinsman on his mother's side.

Saint Luke tells the story of Gabriel's appearance to Zacharias, husband of Elizabeth, in considerable detail. Zacharias and his wife were godly people who had lived a blameless life, but they had never had children. Now both were old. Elizabeth had lost all hope of ever having a baby. When the angel appeared to Zacharias as he was offering incense on the altar in the temple and told him that his wife would have a son, Zacharias could not believe it. "I'm an old man," he said, "and my wife is well advanced in years. How, then, can this be?"

The angel assured him that the prediction would come true. He added that because Zacharias had doubted, he would lose the power of speech and remain dumb until after the promised event had happened. This punishment was instantaneous. When Zacharias came out of the temple, he could not speak a word, and this affliction lasted until after Elizabeth's child was born.

It continued until the time came to name the new baby. Elizabeth said that she wanted the child to be named John, and this puzzled her friends. "None of your relative has that name," they said. "Why don't you name him Zacharias, after his father?" They made signs to Zacharias, trying to find out his preference in the matter. The old man asked for a writing tablet. When it was brought, he wrote down what the angel had told him: "His name is John." Immediately, says the Bible, he was able to speak freely. "And the child grew, and waxed strong in spirit, and was in the deserts till the day of his showing unto Israel."

Meantime Mary, the gentle virgin of Nazareth, had had to tell her fiance, Joseph the carpenter, that she was with child. How did he react to this almost unbelievable story? Saint Matthew's Gospel says that at first he was inclined to break off their engagement. He wanted to do this quietly, so that Mary would not be made "a public example." But then, in a dream, an angel told Joseph not to hesitate to marry Mary, because the child she was carrying had indeed been conceived by the Holy Spirit. And Joseph, too, was obedient to the voice of the angel, knowing that it was also the voice of God.

In those days the Roman emperor, Caesar Augustus, ruled most of the known world. His legions, feared and hated, enforced Pax Romana—the Roman peace—everywhere. Now the emperor ordered a census taken throughout his vast conquered territories. Every man was ordered to return to his native city to be counted. As a descendant of David, Joseph had to return to Bethlehem, the town where David himself had been born a thousand years earlier. He made the journey from Nazareth, taking with him "Mary, his espoused wife, being great with child."

Everyone knows the immortal story of how the weary travelers found shelter in a stable because there was no room for them in the inn. Some say this stable was actually a cave where domestic animals were kept. In

this humble place, with no help, no attendants other than her husband, Mary "brought forth her firstborn son, and wrapped him in swaddling clothes, and laid him in a manger."

Ever since that luminous night, marvelous stories have clustered around it. Best loved, perhaps , is Saint Luke's account of the "shepherds abiding in the field, keeping watch over their flock by night." Even the dullest imagination is thrilled by his description of a sky full of angels singing what was really the first Christmas carol, a promise of peace on earth that all men hope will be fulfilled some day.

Imagine the feeling of those shepherds, simple, honest men, as standing there under the stars they heard the most heavenly music that ever fell upon mortal ears. No wonder they "came with haste" to "see this thing which is come to pass which the Lord hath made known unto us." Countless artists have tried to depict the scene, the roughly clad men kneeling beside the manger, their faces alight with adoration. In a way, those shepherds represent what all of us feel at Christmas time: wonder and reverence mixed with gratitude and joy, the indescribable blend of emotions that for the lack of better words we call the Christmas spirit.

And then there were the Wise Men from

the east, the ones Saint Matthew tells us about. Tradition has it that there were three of them, although the Bible does not mention three or any other number. Legend has even given them names: Caspar, Balthazar, Melchior. Apparently they were astronomers, or perhaps astrologers. Watching the heavens, they had seen the star, or "the rising of his star," as one authority describes the great event.

Many persons have tried to explain the blazing star that "went before" the Wise Men. Some claim that it was a comet, others that it was an unusual conjunction of two or even three planets. I read a gentle fantasy once in which the star was a very small angel who could make himself glow in the dark. This very small angel saw that the camels bearing the Wise Men were straying off course, so he turned himself into a beacon to guide them. It's an explanation that has more appeal, perhaps, than the scientific ones. Whatever it was, the star has become the symbol of hope and gladness at Christmas time. Every year it shines from the tops of countless Christmas trees, just as it glows in the hearts of men.

The Wise Men had brought gifts for the baby: gold, frankincense, myrrh. They went first to the palace of Herod, the wicked king whom the Romans permitted to rule over that territory. Their reading of the stars had told them that a king had been born. Perhaps they assumed that such a child would be brought to the ruler's court.

When Herod heard what the Wise Men had to say, the news threw him into a panic. He was afraid that this newborn king might someday push him off his throne. He tried to trick the Wise Men into telling him where to find the baby. When he failed, he ordered his soldiers to kill all children two years old and under in the Bethlehem area, so the Christ child was in mortal danger from the start. But the Bible says that an angel appeared to Joseph in a dream and warned him to flee with his wife and baby into Egypt. There they stayed until Herod was dead and the danger past.

By modern calculation, Herod died in 4 B.C., and so our system of labeling dates either B.C. or A.D. is probably inaccurate by five or six years. When the custom of indicating dates began, hundreds of years ago, its originator did not possess the historical data available to modern scholars.

So we do not know the exact day or the exact year when Christ came into the world. Perhaps it doesn't matter. What matters is that every year we try to recapture the love and wonder and hope and joy that were born in human hearts when God Himself came into the world to share the mystery and miracle of life with human beings—and to offer them a place in His own eternal kingdom.

No wonder the story comes ringing down the corridors of time with its magic and its message undimmed by the passage of years. Through all the preceding centuries, as the Bible relates, God has tried every other way to get through to man. He sent angels; He spoke through prophets; He made great promises to men like Abraham and Isaac; He revealed Himself to Moses. Yet it was almost as if the concept of God as revealed in all these ways was too overwhelming for the average man to comprehend. So God said to Himself, "I know what I'll do. I'll stop trying to reach them with thunder and lightning, commandments and revelations. I won't send floods or fires anymore, or earthquakes or even a still, small voice. This time I'll send them something so simple, so natural, so lovable that even the densest, the least attentive, the most indifferent will be able to understand. This time I'll send them a baby." And in the form of a baby God laid Himself on the doorstep of the world. And the heart of that world responded to a baby's low cry.

So that baby, who was also King and Savior of the world, was born in a stable in a little town called Bethlehem— and the world has never been the same since.

The Early Years

The Bible tells us very little about the childhood of Jesus. Apparently the authors of the four gospels were so intent on reporting the ministry of the Man from Galilee that they focused their attention almost exclusively on the last three years of his life. Even today these tremendous events make such a deep impression on most of us that we hardly ever stop to visualize Jesus as a small boy.

And yet, we know he was one. We know that since he was completely human as well as completely divine, there must have been times when he played tag or hide-and-seek with children his own age. There may have been times when he got into mischief and perhaps was scolded occasionally.

What about his schooling? Again, we can only guess. Probably it was limited by the need to help Joseph in the carpenter's shop, fashioning household furniture, agricultural tools, yokes for oxen ("my yoke is easy, and my burden is light"). No doubt he helped build houses and thus learned the importance of solid foundations (the "wise man, which built his house upon a rock").

He belonged to a devout family. As a son of the synagogue, he learned to read the scriptures and speak in Hebrew, although Aramaic was the language the family used in everyday affairs. Perhaps he could also speak the common Greek that—like English today— was the international language of the ancient world. From the hills behind Nazareth he could look out over the ancient plain of Esdraelon, where caravans of plodding camels went swaying along and Roman legions came clanking down the roads, their armor flashing in the sun. Surely a child as bright and inquisitive and active as Jesus would have had some contact with these travelers. Inevitably he would have picked up stories and bits of information and phrases in strange tongues.

Nazareth was a very ordinary town; people used to say scornfully, "Can there any good thing come out of Nazareth?" And so some people have wondered how such a mighty intellect could grow in such un-promising soil. Perhaps, so it has been speculated, Jesus studied in some great center of learning—in Egypt, or Greece, or even India. After all, they point out, we do not know exactly where he was or what he did between the ages of twelve and approximately thirty.

But it is not necessarily environment that makes a genius; it's a quality of mind and heart. The young Jesus did not have to go to any special school. All around him was the stuff that life is made of; he simply saw it more vividly and more truly than anyone else. Everywhere he looked, farmers were tending their crops ("and a sower went forth to sow"), and flocks of sheep were grazing ("I am the good shepherd"), and vineyards were filled with workers ("I am the vine, ye are the branches"). Wild poppies grew on the hillsides ("consider the lilies of the field"). Every day was full of little dramas—a housewife losing a coin and searching her whole house for it, a marketplace rumor of a traveler assaulted by robbers and left for

dead, the tale of the village gossip that so-and-so has returned to his father's house penniless and penitent after running away. Of such things, later on, were made the unforgettable stories and parables and illustrations ("never man spake like this man").

Only once do we get a firsthand glimpse of Jesus during his childhood. When he was twelve years old his family made their annual pilgrimage to Jerusalem for the Passover. When the ceremonies were over, they started home with a large group of other pilgrims. Evidently Jesus, as a responsible child, was given quite a large measure of freedom. So his parents were not too concerned when he did not join them; they thought he was with other members of the group. One day's journey from Jerusalem, though, when it became apparent that the boy was not with the caravan, his mother and

Joseph became alarmed. They hurried back to Jerusalem, looking and asking everywhere. The Bible says that they searched for three days (perhaps this meant a day's journey toward Nazareth, a day's journey returning, and one day in Jerusalem). They finally found the boy in one of the porticos of the temple where the rabbis met to discuss all sorts of abstract questions and fine points of religion. There was Jesus "sitting in the midst of the doctors, both hearing them, and asking them questions. And all that heard him were astonished at his understanding and answers."

When his mother asked him why he remained behind, his reaction was one of genuine astonishment that they didn't know where to look for him. The Bible says that he told them he had to be "about my Father's business." It is significant that in these first recorded words of Jesus, he refers to God as his Father. It was a relationship that was to be central to his whole later message and ministry.

His agitated parents, Saint Luke tells us, "understood not the saying which he spake unto them." Evidently there was a bit of a generation gap even in those days! The whole purpose of the story as related is to show that very early in his life Jesus had a strong curiosity about religion, a burning interest in man's relationship to God, and a growing sense, even at that age, of being *different* from other people.

His mother, who was closer to him than any other person, sensed this difference too. The Bible says that after Jesus returned home with his parents and "was subject unto them"—that is, loving and obedient—Mary did not forget what had happened, but "kept all these sayings in her heart."

Thus we are given a vivid glimpse of a growing boy, eager, enthusiastic, hungry for knowledge, full of the love of life. Then the curtains close and we do not see him again for almost twenty years.

The Baptism of Jesus

On a grassy slope near a quiet river a bizarre but impressive figure is preaching. Crowds of city dwellers have come out to this lonely place to hear him, drawn by his compelling eloquence. His hearers are dressed in conventional linen garments and headdresses, but the preacher is clad in a rough shirt made of camel's hide with the hair still on it. He has a leather belt around his waist and crude sandals on his feet. His hair and beard are long; his voice is powerful and resonant. His eyes have a piercing quality, as if they can see through the exterior of any man or woman to the secret thoughts and desires within. The place is the valley of the river Jordan. The time is the fifteenth year of the reign of the Roman Emperor Tiberius.

This strange individual is John, son of Zacharias. We know the circumstances of his birth, but we have not glimpsed him in this Bible story for thirty years. In that time, somehow, he has become a man of God, a prophet in the great tradition that stretches back to Moses. Probably the call came to him in solitude after long meditation in desert places: the Bible says he lived on locusts and wild honey. Now, in the prophetic tradition, he is calling upon his listeners to repent, give up their sins, turn away from evil thoughts and ways, throw themselves on the mercy of

God. To those who are willing to do this he offers a symbolic cleansing: baptism in the River Jordan.

The crowd listens, spellbound, as he attacks evil in high places and low. He speaks out againt Herod, the cowardly and corrupt tetrarch of Galilee whom the Romans permit to govern under their all powerful control. He condemns Herod for his cruelty, his personal immorality, his indifference to justice. His listeners look at one another in amazement: this sort of talk can cause a man to be arrested, imprisoned, even executed.

Now the speaker turns his anger on the two most prominent religious sects of the day: the Pharisees and Sadducees, and the hypocrisy of their leaders—a generation of vipers, he calls them. John believes that their obsession with rules and regulations, with the petty points of theology, is weakening the people's faith in God. We have seen, in our own day, what happens when theologians and theoreticians drain the warmth and vitality out of religion. The churches grow sterile, the people drift away, because man is a feeling as well as a thinking creature. He cannot live by the bitter bread of intellect alone. It was true two thousand years ago. It's still true today.

John knows this. So he lashes out at the

smug assumption of these people that simply being descendents of Abraham makes them better than anyone else. The crowd listens uneasily but intently. Those of us who sometimes address large audiences know that there are two infallible ways to rivet the attention of your audience. One is to tell them they are marvelous. The other is to tell them they are terrible. John the Baptist favors the second technique—and he is very good at it!

But John does not harangue his audience constantly. He welcomes questions and interruptions. "Just hold up your hand," he says, "if there is something on your mind or heart."

And the hands go up. A bearded man near the front of the crowd has a worried look. "I'm a tax collector," he says. "I know everyone despises me. And yet the Romans insist that taxes be collected. What can I do to win the kind of salvation you speak of?"

The fierce eyes regard him with sudden gentleness. "Do your job honestly. Don't use it to extort money from people. Greed and dishonesty keep a man from the kingdom of God, not the job of collecting taxes."

Now an off-duty soldier, trying to be inconspicuous, hears himself speak up. "What about us? We're hated too."

"People are afraid of you with good reason. So don't take advantage of your authority. Don't loot or steal. Be content with your wages." The eagle eyes sweep around the crowd. "You must learn, all of you, to give, not get. Those who have must share with those who have not. If you own two coats and you meet a man who has none, give him one of yours..."

The strong voice falls silent momentarily as a tall figure on the edge of the throng moves forward. John speaks softly, almost to himself: "Behold the Lamb of God, who taketh away the sin of the world..."

Once more in this, the greatest story ever told, Jesus moves into our view.

Did John know Jesus by sight: I'm sure he did. While Jesus was growing up in Galilee, John was reaching his own manhood not far away in the hills of Judea. Doubtless the two families exchanged visits, or met for ceremonial occasions in Jerusalem. The two cousins, so close in age if not in temperment, must have known each other well.

What were their conversations like as carefree teenagers or later as serious young men? Did they talk of the future that held so much tragedy and triumph for both of them? Did they compare their ideas about religion: Did they agree that the traditional faith of the people was being cramped and limited by religious hair-splittings and formalisms of all kinds? Did they also agree to try, someday, to do something about it?

We don't know. All we know is that the two cousins were born under miraculous circumstances. Both had a passionate sense of man's destiny as a child of God. Both were to display utter fearlessness in denouncing evil, both were to preach with an eloquence never heard before or since. And both were to end their earthly lives by dying cruelly and unjustly at the hands of the civil authorities.

Of the two young men, John was the first to come to public attention. But as his fame spread—and it spread swiftly—he steadfastly refused to take credit for being anything or anyone he was not. When people asked if he were the expected Messiah, or even some reincarnation of the prophet Elijah, he emphatically denied it. His mission, he kept insisting, was to tell the people about Someone who was to follow him: "He that cometh after me is mightier than I, whose shoes I am not worthy to bear."

Did John know that this "Someone" was to be his own kinsman? Saint Matthew's Gospel hints that he did, because it says that when Jesus came to John to be baptized, John told him that their roles should be reversed, that he should be seeking baptism from Jesus. On the other hand, Saint John's Gospel seems to indicate that John recognized Jesus as the Messiah only at the moment when he baptized him and saw the Holy Spirit "descending from heaven like a dove, and it abode upon him."

In any case, all four gospels make it clear that when Jesus came out of the river after being baptized by John, absolute conviction had come to both of them from God Himself that this unknown young man from Nazareth was indeed the Savior whose coming had been predicted for so many centuries.

Why did Jesus in whom there was no sin, choose to be baptized? Jesus told John, somewhat cryptically, to "suffer it to be so now: for thus it becometh us to fulfill all righteousness." But perhaps Jesus wanted to begin his ministry with a public act of reverence and submission to God's will, whatever that will for him might be.

Once he had made this gesture, there could be no turning back.

The Great Drama Begins

Very often, after some great emotional experience, there is a need to be alone. To relive and rethink the experience. To determine how it has changed things, and ponder what those changes mean. To allow the drained mind and the exhausted spirit to regain poise and strength. To seek deep self-knowledge undistracted by other people. After the tremendous experience of his baptism, this solitude was what Jesus needed.

He went away by himself into the wilderness, where he fasted for forty days and forty nights. A symbolic length of time, perhaps; Moses fasted forty days, as did Elijah. Despite the symbolic discipline of Lent, fasting is no longer widely practiced in our own materialistic day. But the Bible makes it clear that there is enormous spiritual power in it, that it gives a great sense of mastery over self as well as clarity of mind and deep religious insight.

Why did Jesus resort to this ancient practice? Perhaps because, being human as well as divine, he had to make up his mind about his mission, about what he was going to do next and how he was going to do it. He was the long-expected Messiah—a shattering revelation to the human side of him. How was he to handle this stupendous assignment? What was he to do first? What was his Father's ultimate will for him? Who

would help him? What road should he follow? How should he use the enormous powers that now were his to command?

Perhaps this last question was the most difficult of all. Jesus knew that the power that had been given to him was indeed absolute. The Devil knew it too, and it was in this area that he launched his attack—just as he always picks a potentially vulnerable spot in which to launch his attack on anyone.

The first temptation was partly physical. The Bible says that after his long fast, Jesus was desperately hungry. "If thou be the Son of God," the tempted said, "command that these stones be made bread." A diabolically clever proposal! Not only would Jesus' gnawing hunger be appeased, he would have instant corroboration of what his baptism had led him to believe about himself. Perhaps the human side of Jesus still had some doubts. Satan's use of that word "if" shows how clever he was—and is—at destroying faith. He was trying to destroy one of the foundations of Christianity—faith—before it even got started, by implanting doubt in the giver of the message himself.

But, as he had been taught as a young boy, Jesus met the challenge of evil by confronting it with the word of God. He quoted Deuteronomy 8:3. "It is written," he said,

"Man shall not live by bread alone, but by every word that proceedeth out of the mouth of God."

The second temptation was deadlier still. Jesus had a burning desire to reach all men with the message that God loved them. What quicker way to do this than to perform some feat so spectacular that no one who saw it or heard about it would be able to doubt his word? If he jumped from the top of the temple and floated gently to the ground before hundreds of astounded witnesses, the result might be the instant conversion of all.

But Jesus knew that the end can never justify the means if the means are unworthy. Again he quoted Deuteronomy: "It is written again, Thou shall not tempt the Lord thy God."

Finally, the Bible says, the tempter took Jesus up to the top of a very high mountain, showed him all the kingdoms of the world, and offered them to him for a price—the price of losing his own soul. Ambition is a characteristic of strong men, and in Jesus was a personality that ultimately was to prove stronger than death. But again he parried the tempter's thrust with a quotation from Scripture: "Get thee hence, Satan: for it is written, Thou shalt worship the Lord thy God, and him only shalt thou serve."

Three times, significantly, Jesus used those words, "It is written," to justify the decisions that he made. Surely there is a message here for all of us: that strength and wisdom are to be found in the written word of God, and that wise men and women will saturate themselves with it in order to meet the challenge of evil, no matter what form it takes in their lives.

By the time he came out of the wilderness, Jesus knew what he was going to do. He would use his miraculous powers, but only to help others or to gain acceptance of his message. He would need a small group of dedicated, faithful men to help him spread the gospel—the good news—and carry on his work after he had returned to the Father Who had sent him. He knew that what he intended to do—revolutionize religion—would bring him into direct conflict with the narrow-minded men who considered themselves the nation's spiritual leaders. Knowing human nature as he did, he foresaw that they would eventually use the lethal power of Rome in their attempts to destroy him. It would not take many months or years for them to bring this about. He knew he had very little time.

His first move, therefore, was to recruit the little bank of chosen and trusted lieutenants that he knew he would need. How did he do this? Simply by asking them! What magnetism, what charm, what irresistible appeal he must have had! We don't know what he looked like. The Bible, strangely, gives us no hint at all. But perhaps this is just as well—each of us is free to imagine his appearance. I think, myself, that he was tall and strong, bronzed from tramping those primitive roads under the fierce desert sun. I think he must have had marvelous eyes, full of humor and kindness, but with a piercing quality, too. How else can we account for the reactions of the disciples? Peter and Andrew were fishermen and loved their work. But Jesus said to them (and I'm sure he was smiling as he said it), "Follow me, and I will make you fishers of men." And "they straightway left their nets, and followed him." Why? Because that smile charmed them right out of their boats!

Or take the case of Matthew, the tax collector. He had a good job. He probably loved money, since collecting it was his business. He was in a position to feather his nest whenever he wanted by squeezing a little more money out of the taxpayers who, after all, were not going to complain too loudly for fear of the power of Rome. There he was, sitting at his table with all his money and his papers (tax forms of some kind, even as now) and his little bureaucratic sense of self-importance, when suddenly a stranger passes by. The stranger halts for half a second. He evaluates Matthew in one lightning glance that tells him all he needs to know, all there *is* to know, about this man. He looks once into Matthew's eyes. "Follow me!" he says. No preliminaries. No explanations. Just two words. "And," says the Bible, "he arose, and followed him."

Once that experience happened to a man, he was never the same again. That Jesus knew this is indicated by his changing Simon's name to Peter—and again I think he was smiling when he did it. An affectionate nickname, based on the rugged physical strength of the big fisherman, but also with an ultimate spiritual significance. Simon the Rock. A solid sound!

"Follow me!" He said it to twelve men...and he is still saying it to all of us.

Now the cast of characters was complete. Now the great drama could begin.

The Miracles

Everybody loves a wedding. Always there's a sense of solemnity: two young people pledging their lives to each other, come what may. There's always a touch of wistfulness, too, as the spectators recall their own wedding days, bright with hopes and great expectations. Often there are tears, welling out of a deep sense of life fulfilling itself. But once the ceremony is over, the dominant mood is one of gaiety. People want to celebrate—and they do.

Suppose you lived some twenty centuries ago in a little town in Galilee called Cana, Suppose you were invited to a wedding. You'd go, wouldn't you? You'd wear your best clothes and your best smile and you'd congratulate the happy pair. You'd expect refreshments: cakes and wine, fresh fruit perhaps, raisins and dates, all sorts of delectable things.

In a small town, you'd know most of the guests. The young men would be watching the pretty girls. The pretty girls would be interested in eligible bachelors. At this wedding there are quite a few. Among the guests are Jesus, son of Joseph, and some of the young men he has been recruiting recently for some purpose or other, you're not quite sure what.

It's a splendid wedding; everyone is having a fine time, when suddenly the wine supply gives out. Perhaps more guests were invited than the host realized. Or perhaps an expected delivery from the wine merchant failed to materialize. Now there's great consternation among the families of the bride and groom. It looks as if they're going to be acutely embarrassed.

Among the guests is a stately woman with a lovely face: Mary, wife of Joseph, mother of Jesus. No doubt she's a close friend of the mother of the bride. Anyway, she knows about the problem. You hear her speak to her son in an agitated whisper: "Isn't this terrible? They're out of wine!" You can't quite hear her son's reply, but she looks relieved. She beckons to a servant and tells him to do whatever her son commands.

Nearby are six large stone jars, each capable of holding twenty or thirty gallons. You see the servants fill each of them with fresh, clear water. "Now," you hear Jesus say to them, "draw some out and take it to the steward of the feast."

Intrigued, you watch the steward accept the cup and taste the contents. His face brightens with astonishment and pleasure. Obviously, he thinks the wine merchant has made his delivery after all. He shouts jovially to the bridegroom, "You're a sly fellow! Most people serve the best wine first, but you've kept the best for the last!" He orders this marvelous vintage served to everyone. The party goes on more joyously than ever.

But you are still puzzled. You tap one of the servants on the shoulder. "What did you pour into those jars? Wasn't it water? Is this some sort of joke or trick?"

The servant gives a despairing shrug. "No joke. No trick. We don't know what that man did. It's all very strange!"

He hurries away, looking almost frightened. Still baffled, you go over to one of the jars that is still full. The ruby-colored liquid has a wonderful bouquet; the air around it seems perfumed. You glance around to see if anyone is watching. No one is, so you dip a surreptitious finger into the jar and touch it to your lips. Superb! The best wine you have ever tasted. But how can this be? A few moments ago it was water. You saw it yourself.

You look across the room. Jesus is standing beside his mother, talking easily with some of the guests, smiling his radiant smile. And suddenly something strikes your consciousness like the deep, vibrating note of an invisible gong. It's no joke. It's no trick. This man is like no other person you ever saw or ever will see. This man is... *different*.

The miracle at Cana, the Bible tells us, was the first that Jesus performed after he returned from Judea into Galilee. There's a hint that he had not intended to use his supernatural powers so soon, that he was not quite ready. But when he saw that his hosts were upset, and that his gentle mother felt sorry for them, he put aside his own timetable and his own preference.

How human and how marvelous—marvelous that the first public manifestation of this stupendous force was directed toward

the solution of a minor social problem! Use the infinite power of God Almighty to sustain the mood of merriment at a small-town wedding reception? Jesus seems to be saying, with that wonderful smile, "Why not? You are all God's children. He wants you to be happy. So why not?"

From that day forward, over the next three years, a series of events took place that dwarfed the remarkable happening at Cana. Events that defied all known laws of cause and effect. Events that transcended everything that medical science knew then or knows now. Events that time and again swept away the barriers between the material and the spiritual worlds.

How can the limited human mind explain a person who can cure insanity with a word, heal leprosy or blindness with a touch, walk on water, calm a raging storm, bring the dead back to life? The answer is simple: it can't. Reason falters. The only path to understanding is faith.

In some of the miracles, it's true, we can see Jesus, the master psychologist, at work. Modern medicine has come to believe that there is no clear-cut, hard-and-fast line between mind and body; both are inseparable parts of the same entity. Time and again the New Testament gives proof that Jesus of Nazareth was fully aware of this two thousand years ago.

Take the case of the sick man at the pool of Bethesda, for example. Saint John writes about it clearly and decisively. When you read his words you know that this was no hearsay, no secondhand report. John was there. He saw what happened. He heard what was said.

"Now there is at Jerusalem by the sheep market a pool, which is called in the Hebrew tongue Bethesda, having five porches. In these lay a great multitude of impotent folk, of blind, halt, withered, waiting for the moving of the water. For an angel went down at a certain season into the pool, and troubled the water: whosoever then first after the troubling of the water stepped in was made whole of whatsoever disease he had."

The pool at Bethesda has been excavated and may be seen in Jerusalem today, some twenty feet below present ground level. It is fed by a spring whose action caused the intermittent "troubling" or bubbling of the water. This was the site that Christ chose for one of his most fascinating demonstrations of healing.

The sick man had been lying there, the Bible says, for thirty-eight years. The implication, surely, is that he had not made very strenuous efforts to be the first into the pool after it had bubbled. Perhaps, like some modern invalids, he enjoyed the notoriety gained by such a sustained record of poor health. Jesus evidently thought so, for the first thing he said to the man was "Do you want to be cured?"

Now most normal people would have said, "I certainly do." But this man could not bring himself to ask for healing. If he were healed, how could he go on "enjoying" poor health? So he started giving excuses about not being able to get into the water quickly at the proper time.

Jesus knew that if this state of mind were allowed to persist, the man would never change. So he brushed the excuses aside. "Rise!" he said, in his firm, no-nonsense voice. "Take up thy bed, and walk!" With those commanding eyes fixed on him, the sick man had no choice. A current of power flowed into him, so strong, so irresistible, that thirty-eight years of self-absorption melted away. He stood up. He picked up his bed. He carried it away.

Later, meeting the man again, Jesus said to him, "Behold, thou art made whole: sin no more, lest a worse thing come unto thee." What sin had the man committed? We don't know, but it doesn't matter. What matters is the relationship that Jesus stresses here between ill health and wrongdoing. Sometimes when illness comes it is not the victim's fault at all; Jesus made that clear when asked about a man who was born blind.

But sometimes there is a connection between the way a person lives and thinks and acts and the way that person feels. Sustained wrong-thinking, wrong-acting, wrong-feeling can make you sick. Immorality seems to block the health-giving life-force that comes from God.

John's Gospel goes on to describe many subsequent miracles of Jesus, astounding events that seem to defy the laws of nature as we understand them. One of these mighty deeds made such an impression on his contemporaries that it is described in all four Gospels, It involved a great crowd of five thousand people who had gathered on a remote hillside near the Sea of Galilee to hear Jesus. All day they had listened to him, fascinated. Now night was drawing on, and the disciples asked Jesus to send the crowd away so that the people would be able to find food in neighboring villages.

"Why don't you feed them?" Jesus suggested, knowing well what they would say.

"Because we don't have any food," they answered. "Even if we spent what little money we have, it wouldn't be enough."

"Does anyone have any food?" asked Jesus quietly.

Andrew, Peter's brother, spoke up. "There's a lad here who has five barley loaves and two small fishes."

"Bring them to me," Jesus said. When they were brought, he raised his eyes to heaven and gave thanks. Then he had the people sit down on the grassy slopes in groups of fifty or a hundred. This meant that there were about eight or ten groups, so that each could be served by one or two persons.

Jesus gave each disciple a basket with a portion of the food in it. Then they moved through the ranks of seated people. Perhaps Jesus served one group himself, handing out portions of fish and bread, smiling into the

grateful, upturned faces. And gradually gratitude turned to amazement and awe, because no matter how much food was handed out, there was always more in the basket. The hungry people ate, and no doubt some asked for and received second helpings, but the supply—like the love of God, which indeed it was—never grew less. When this amazing meal was over, Jesus had the disciples pick up fragments of food so that nothing would be wasted. And John's gospel says that they filled twelve baskets with broken pieces of the five barley loaves that were left over after the hungry people had finished.

Twelve baskets of fragments from five small loaves! The people were astounded. John reports that when they saw this sign of Jesus' power they kept saying, "This surely is the Prophet who was to come into the world!"

How can we dwellers in the twentieth century explain such a thing? We can't. We can only believe that it happened. Modern science tells us that underneath the familiar appearances that surround us—tables, chairs, loaves, fishes—everything is composed of billions of whirling electrical particles. No one understands how the invisible power called mind can affect these ultimate entities. But, Jesus of Nazareth knew.

This unique Person could also control the forces of nature that we call weather. Once, when the disciples and the Master were crossing the Sea of Galilee in a small boat, a furious storm arose. That inland sea can become very rough very quickly. While the disciples struggled and rowed and bailed,

Jesus slept peacefully in the stern. At last, convinced that the boat was sinking, they woke him up and begged him to save them. Raising his head, Jesus spoke calmly to the raging winds and seas: "Peace! Be still!" And instantly the storm ceased.

On another occasion, when the disciples were in the boat on a stormy night, they saw a dim figure approaching. It was Jesus, walking on the surface of the sea, on his way to join them. They were terrified, thinking that they were seeing an apparition or a ghost. But he reassured them, saying, "Don't be afraid. It is I." A wonderful story, reminding us that Christ can always come to any of us, no matter how fierce the storms of life may be.

St. Matthew's Gospel says that Peter recognizing the Lord, cried, "If it's really you, tell me to come to you on the water!"

"Come on, then," Jesus replied. Peter jumped out of the boat and for a few steps he did walk on the water. But then as the black waves surged around him he panicked and began to sink. Jesus reached out and caught him, reproaching him gently for his lack of faith. When the two of them were back in the boat, the whole crew came and knelt before Jesus, hailing him as the Son of God.

Of all the mighty miracles that Jesus wrought, the ones that left his contemporaries most awestruck were those in which he displayed his mastery over the thing we call death. In all the long course of history, no person had ever returned, once that final boundary was crossed. But on more than one occasion Jesus brought such people back to life.

The most dramatic of these episodes took

place in the little town of Bethany, scarcely two miles from Jerusalem. Here three of Jesus' dearest friends lived, Mary and Martha and their brother, Lazarus, When Lazarus became seriously ill, the first thought his sisters had was to send for Jesus, who was in Galilee. They had seen him heal people as sick as their brother, or sicker. They had complete faith that he could make Lazarus well.

But Jesus did not respond to their summons right away; "he abode two days still in the same place where he was." His disciples were sorry to hear that Lazarus was ill, but they had no desire to go into Judea, where by now the opponents of Jesus were actively seeking to destroy him. Their fears were so great that when Jesus finally told them that he was going to Bethany, Thomas said resignedly to the other disciples, "Let us also go, that we may die with him." Thomas knew that Herod had persecuted John the Baptist. He knew what could happen to

prophets and their followers. But they were ready to follow Jesus to the end.

To this day, in the ancient village of Bethany, time seems to stand still. The ruins of the house where Lazarus and his sisters are said to have lived are still there. So is a tomb said to be thè tomb of Lazarus himself.

The Bible tells us that when Jesus approached Bethany, Lazarus had been buried for four days. Many friends of the two sisters had gathered "to comfort them concerning their brother." When word came that Jesus was approaching the village, Mary stayed at home, numb with grief, but Martha ran to meet the Master. "Lord," she said to him, weeping, "if thou hadst been here, my brother had not died."

Jesus told her gently that her brother would rise again. She thought he meant that Lazarus would be included in the resurrection of all souls at the end of time. But Jesus made his meaning clear in words that are the most thrilling in all Scripture: "I am the resurrection, and the life: he that believeth in me, though he were dead, yet shall he live: and whosoever liveth and believeth in me shall never die."

What a stupendous promise! What a staggering statement! But Martha accepted it without doubt or question. "Believest thou this?" Jesus asked her searchingly. "Yea, Lord," she answered. "I believe..."

Perhaps that unquestioning faith had something to do with the incredible thing that happened next. Jesus, the Bible says, was upset as he came to the sealed grave. He wept—and the people who stood by whispered to one another, "See how much he loved Lazarus." Finally he ordered the stone to be removed from the entrance to the tomb.

Again, all the details of scene and the dialogue are so clear and sharp that they must have been set down by an eyewitness. Ever the realistic one of the two sisters, Martha warns that the body has been buried for four days and that opening the tomb may be unpleasant. But Jesus reminds her of her own faith. "Said I not unto thee, that, if thou wouldest believe, thou shouldest see the glory of God?"

He looked up to heaven as if gathering all his strength. He said a prayer. Then in a mighty voice of command he cried, "Lazarus, come forth!" And, says the Bible, in words that make this awesome scene chilling still,

"he that was dead came forth, bound hand and foot with grave clothes, and his face was bound about with a napkin."

Imagine the stunned silence that fell upon the crowd as that ghostly figure moved from the shadowed doorway into the sunshine. Some, I am sure, fell on their knees. Some no doubt ran away. Imagine too, the joy, the stupefaction, the incredulity on the faces of the two sisters. Then Jesus' voice, exhausted perhaps, but calm and reassuring: "Loose him, and let him go."

I have stood, myself, outside that ancient tomb in Bethany. I have gone down the twenty-two steps to the place, hewn out of rock, where the body of Lazarus is said to have lain. And I have felt my heart grow warm and my eyes fill with tears as an overwhelming conviction swept over me: that God's answer to the riddle of existence is not death. It is life.

I believe this because I believe the promise of the One who also said, "I am come that they might have life, and that they might have it more abundantly."

The Greatest Stories Ever Told

Even if Jesus had never performed a single miracle, huge crowds would have gathered just to listen to him. As a speaker, as a teacher, as a storyteller, he had no equal. Over and over the Bible says that "the common people heard him gladly." At times they thronged so closely about him that he had to get into a boat and talk to them from a few yards offshore.

Even his enemies were fascinated and spellbound. At one point the Pharisees sent soldiers to arrest Jesus. They found him all right, but they came back empty-handed. "Why didn't you seize him?" the Pharisees demanded angrily. The soldiers looked sheepishly at one another. Finally one muttered, "Never man spake like this man." The soldier was right. No man had ever talked the way Jesus talked. And no man since has ever talked with such charm and persuasiveness.

I know from my own experience that to communicate effectively with large groups of people, several things are necessary. You must know your audience—know what interests them, what will touch their hearts and minds, what will help them. You must be clear in your own mind about the message you are trying to give, and sincere in your own belief in it. Finally, as an old actor once told me, you must love your audience, you must care about them as individuals. If you love them, they will sense it and respond. Since Jesus Christ was love incarnate, his hearers must have found themselves surrounded and permeated by love.

The parables—the stories that Jesus told to illustrate his teachings—have become a priceless part of the world's literature.

Simple, vivid, apt, they were passed from person to person by word of mouth and finally written down years after Jesus' human life was ended. Let's take one of the most famous and best loved of all the parables—the story of the Good Samaritan—and try to analyze some of the ingredients that made this type of teaching so effective.

One remarkable thing about this story is that is was absolutely spontaneous. Jesus didn't ponder it for a long time and write it down or rewrite it. He just told it in answer to a somewhat unfriendly question. What an answer it was!

The Bible, as usual, sets the scene for us vividly. A certain lawyer has been testing Jesus with questions designed more to display his own erudition than anything else. In the course of the conversation he asks Jesus to define the word *neighbor*. Jesus offers no abstract or hair-splitting definition. He simply tells a story out of his own matchless imagination, that for drama and suspense and conciseness is a master-piece.

Look at the opening of the story and see how much is accomplished in a single sentence. "A certain man" Jesus begins, "went down from Jerusalem to Jericho, and fell among thieves..." Instantly his hearers are intrigued. The "certain man" might be any of them, for all of them have traveled the familiar Jerusalem-Jericho road. In thirteen words Jesus has created his main character, placed him in a specific locality, caused his listeners to identify with this character, and injected the key element in any story—suspense.

Already certain reactions are taking place

in the minds of the audience. The hero is in trouble; what will happen to him? How will it all end? This is the oldest theme in the world and the most compelling one: man against death, or the threat of death. The audience wants the hero to escape or be saved. Their attention is riveted on Jesus. They are hooked!

The listeners want a solution right away, but this master storyteller uses a few more words in the first sentence to build up the suspense even more: "which stripped him of his raiment, and wounded him, and departed, leaving him half dead." Look at the action in each of those phrases! In his mind's eye, each member of the listening crowd can see the bandits ambushing the unfortunate traveler, beating him, stripping off his clothes, tossing him bloody and unconscious to the side of the road, then vanishing into the undergrowth themselves.

"And by chance there came down a certain priest that way...." Ah, a possible solution appears. Surely this priest will help; after all, a man of God must be devoted to his fellow man. But wait a minute. "And when he saw him, he passed by on the other side."

Incredible! What kind of priest is this? If the unconscious form of the victim had been hidden in the bushes, there might be some excuse. But it wasn't hidden. He saw him... and ignored him.

Now a little flame of indignation begins to burn in the listener's mind. Something must be wrong with the kind of religion represented by that selfish priest. What a hypocrite! But the story rushes on at a breathless pace. Now the focus comes to rest on another figure moving down the bandit-infested road. "And likewise a Levite, when he was at the place, came and looked on him, and passed by on the other side."

Unbelievable! This Levite is acting even worse than the priest. This proud member of the tribe of Levi, the most saintly of all the tribes of Israel, the one given the assignment of helping the priests care for the tabernacle... this man comes over and stares down at the helpless groaning man. Then he too decides that this is none of his business. He doesn't want to get involved. He looks around apprehensively. If he stays here, the bandits may come after *him*. So he too hurries down the road.

So far, in less than one hundred words, Jesus has created a story with a central character, two secondary characters, several villains, action, drama, suspense, characterization (we know a great deal about the priest and the Levite!)—and deep moral implications. And the climax is still to come.

Now Jesus signals the change from complication of his plot to resolution. He does it by using the single word: "But..." When they hear that "but," the listeners know that something good is about to happen, for a change.

"But a certain Samaritan, as he journeyed, came where he was; and when he saw him, he had compassion on him..." Now the

audience reaction is one of amazement. A certain *who?* Ever since pagan invaders hundreds of years earlier had carried off Jews from the northern part of Palestine, replacing them with foreigners who had intermarried with surviving Jews, these Samaritans—people of mixed blood—had been considered second-class citizens by pure-blooded children of Israel. Was it possible that this marvelous storyteller was about to make one of these despised people the hero of his story? Who ever heard of such a thing?

The question tightens the suspense one more notch. Maybe, the people are saying to themselves, this Samaritan *did* feel a momentary flash of pity. But would he turn aside to help a wounded Jew? Not very likely!

But before you can answer the question, the story has moved on: "And went to him, and bound up his wounds, pouring in oil and wine [notice how precise are the details of this ancient form of antisepsis]...and brought him to an inn, and took care of him..." This Samaritan, this outcast, not only renders temporary first aid, he goes to enormous trouble to see that the hit-and-run victim is brought to a safe place.

"And on the morrow when he departed, he took out two pence [again, the specific amount is the kind of detail that gives the story its enormous credibility], and gave them to the host, and said unto him, 'Take care of him: and whatsoever thou spendest more, when I come again, I will repay thee.'" The compassion of the Samaritan is no casual thing. He spends his time. He spends his money. He spends himself—on a stranger. He commits himself for the future as well as for the present. How many of us today do as much when we attempt an act of kindness?

This marvelous, effortless, impromptu story ends simply as it began. A hush has fallen on the listening crowd. The message is so clear, so unmistakable: those who pretend to be better than their fellow men, those who are holier-than-thou, are not necessarily the best people in the sight of God. Kindness and compassion are not the exclusive possession of any given race or social class—they can be displayed by anyone.

Now, smiling gently, Jesus asks the overbearing lawyer a question that any child could answer: "Which now of these three, thinkest thou, was neighbor unto him who fell among the thieves?"

This lawyer is no longer the intellectual snob that he was. He knows real genius when he sees it and hears it. He answers humbly, "He that showed mercy on him."

And Jesus says to him—and to the rest of the crowd—"Go, and do thou likewise."

Perhaps even more beloved than the story of the Good Samaritan is the parable of the Prodigal Son, which might better be called the parable of the Forgiving Father, since the Bible does not mention the word *prodigal* at all.

This is the story of a well-to-do man who had two sons. The younger boy, impatient and adventurous, asked his father to give him his share of whatever inheritance might be coming to him so that he could leave home and see the world.

The father agreed to do this, and the boy journeyed to "a far country," where he quickly squandered all his money in loose living—wine, women, gambling, every sort of extravagance and folly. Then a famine came to that country. The boy's money ran out. Hungry and desperate, he got a job that consisted of feeding pigs. Soon he found himself eating the scraps that were thrown to the swine.

This miserable existence went on until one day, as the Bible puts it, the boy "came to himself." That is, for the first time since leaving home he really began to think. He realized that he had no one to blame for his predicament but himself. He also realized that the least of his father's servants had plenty to eat and was far better off than he was.

So he decided to do what is often the simplest and yet the most difficult thing to do when a mistake has been made: take the blame and apologize. "I'll go home," he said to himself. "I'll say to my father, 'Father, I have sinned against heaven and before you. I'm no longer worthy to be called your son, but perhaps you will give me a place among the least of your servants.' "

Somehow the boy made his way back to his father's house, wondering if his father would consent to speak to him or even see him. But in his misery and remorse, the boy completely underestimated the depth of his father's affection and the patient selflessness of his love. The father didn't even wait for the boy to come to him. When he saw him coming, while he was "yet a great way off," his father ran and embraced him and kissed him and welcomed him home.

The boy tried to apologize. He uttered the difficult words of self-condemnation that on the long journey home he had learned by heart. But the father brushed these aside. "Bring quickly the best clothing," he told his servants, "and put a ring on his hand and shoes on his feet, and kill the fatted calf, and let us rejoice because my son, who was lost, is found."

The story could almost end there, on this note of forgiveness and happiness. But Jesus, the master storyteller, knew that there was still one loose end: the reaction of the older brother. In a kind of epilogue, that very human reaction is briefly and beautifully described. The older brother comes home. He hears the sound of music and dancing and he asks a servant what is going on. When he learns the truth, he is deeply hurt. After all, he has been a good and faithful son. He has never done anything wrong. He has always obeyed his father. But nobody has killed a calf or made a feast for him. Nobody has brought new robes or put a ring on his finger. Is this fair?

The father does not say that it is "fair." He simply says, "Son, you are always with me, and all that is mine is yours. But it is fitting that we should rejoice and be glad, because your brother was dead, but now he is alive. He was lost, and he is found."

Was the older brother reconciled? We don't know; the Scripture doesn't say. But

Jesus made this same wonderful point in other stories: that there is great rejoicing in Heaven when a lost sheep returns to the fold. And if we are fortunate enough to be among the sheep who have never been lost, we should rejoice too.

These brilliant short stories are only two of many that have been preserved in the four Gospels. Others, no doubt, have also been lost. But we should be thankful for those we have. Anyone who wonders about his own relationship to religion can read the parable of the Sower who sows the word of God, sometimes in good soil, sometimes in bad. Anyone who wonders what the purpose of life is can read the Parable of the Talents. These stories are like burning arrows, winging their way into the human heart.

For three short years the teller of these tales walked the roads of Galilee and Judea, sat on sunny hillsides, spoke to anyone who would listen to him. Then he was gone . . . and there has never been such a storyteller since.

The Death of John the Baptist

As the word of Jesus' astounding miracles spread through the land, as the fame of the Carpenter of Nazareth increased, things were not going so well for his cousin, John the Baptist. John's outspokenness had finally landed him in prison. He might have gotten away with his criticism of Herod, the puppet ruler of Galilee, if he had confined himself to that. But he had also spoken in harsh terms of Herod's wife, Herodias. This strong-minded, evil woman had formerly been married to Herod's brother, Philip. John said sternly that it was not right for Herod to marry his brother's wife. This enraged Herodias. She persuaded her husband to have John arrested, but even this did not satisfy her. She wanted his indignant voice silenced forever. She wanted him dead.

Her opportunity finally came when Herod gave a great banquet to celebrate his own birthday. All the powerful and important people in Galilee were there. Lavish food and drink and entertainment were provided. It happened that Herodias had a beautiful daughter named Salome who was a spectacular dancer. It was decided that Salome should dance before Herod and his guests.

Legend has it that Salome was clad only in gauzy veils that she discarded one by one as she danced. Whether this is true or not, her sensuous performance roused the guests to wild applause. Herod was so pleased that he promised to give his stepdaughter anything she desired, even half his kingdom. "Ask what you will," he cried drunkenly. "You shall have it!" And all his guests heard this foolish promise.

Salome had the body of a woman, but the mind of a child. Certainly she was under her mother's thumb. When she told Herodias about Herod's promise, and asked her what to request, that vengeful woman saw her chance. "I'll tell you exactly what to do," she must have said fiercely. "Ask for the head of John the Baptist to be brought in on a platter. Right now, this minute! This banquet will be one that no one will ever forget!"

Perhaps Salome was horrified. But she was too dominated by her mother even to hesitate. She did what she was told. She stood before Herod and in her childish voice made her bloodthirsty request.

The shouting and laughter died away. This was horrifying, even for those barbaric times. There must have been an unearthly silence in the great hall as every eye turned to Herod. It was well known that although Herod had imprisoned John, he really respected him and liked to listen to him, even though what the prophet said usually upset him. But now he was trapped. A ruler could not go back on his pledged word. Reluctantly, he beckoned to a guard. "Do as she says. Bring me here the head of John the Baptist!"

The prison was not far away. The grisly command was carried out instantly. The platter with its ghastly contents was carried into the hall, from which all merriment had fled. Pale and grim, Herod knew well whose idea this murder was. He watched as the platter was handed to Salome, who took it to her triumphant mother. And Herodias was right: no person who attended that banquet ever forgot it.

When Jesus was told what had happened, the Bible says that he went away by himself. He needed prayer and solitude to sustain him in his grief. He also knew that what had happened to John was an indication of what lay ahead on his own path. But he was determined to follow it to the end.

The Teachings

Along the shore of the Sea of Galilee not far from Capernaum is a low hill sloping gently down to the water's edge.

Here was delivered, on one never-to-be-forgotten day, the greatest speech of all time. Here were spoken certain principles that have lived ever since and live now, for they represent truth, the basic truth that is unchanging.

The speech is called the Sermon on the Mount. The hill is the one referred to by Matthew where Jesus sat and spoke to his disciples. That a great throng was present is hardly to be doubted, for everyone wanted to hear Jesus. He captivated them all. And many people could gather on that wide hillside.

Let us picture the scene. Jesus, as the teacher, is seated and the throngs surrounding him are standing; as was the custom in those times. A teacher was held in high respect, and even an emperor had been known to stand respectfully before the seated scholar. Saint Luke tells us this sermon was given on a "plain," or a level place. And he says a huge crowd gathered around the great teacher, coming not only from the locality but also from many faraway places. Throngs always went to Jesus.

That Matthew locates this sermon on a hill and Luke on level ground is not at all inconsistent, for it is reasonable to suppose that, even as today, a great and popular speaker like Jesus would give the same talk in more than one place.

But where it was given is not nearly so important as the message it contained, the marvelous things he said, and the way he said them. How fortunate anyone was to have been there to hear that musical, far-carrying voice (he needed no public address system!) that could easily be heard by the person farthest removed in the huge crowd. The meadow grass was rippled by a gentle breeze, as it is today on a sun-kissed afternoon. The nearby lake glistened like myriads of diamonds in the bright sunlight. In the distance loomed the hills of Syria. A deep silence rested upon the crowd as they listened raptly to the golden sentences, the immortal truths, as they fell from the Teacher's lips. These persons were hearing, perhaps for the first time, the outline of a way of life that was to guide and help untold millions for twenty centuries and in every part of the world.

There have been many famous speakers in the world, and some speeches can be considered truly great, perhaps immortal. But none even remotely compares to this presentation of the basic truths of life stated so simply, yet with such power, in this famous sermon delivered by Jesus Christ. Judged by its impact upon life and history, it was and remains the supreme speech of all time. The Mount of Beatitudes has become for mankind the place where an authoritative moral code, or even more—a moral ideal—was first promulgated.

The introduction to the Sermon on the Mount is called the Beatitudes. The word *beatitude* comes from the Latin abstract noun *beatitudo,* meaning blessed and happy. In a word, the Beatitudes tell us what kind of person really is blessed and happy. No

person has ever "told it like it is" regarding that state called happiness as did Jesus Christ when he taught the crowds gathered around him on the Mount. And for twenty centuries he has been the acknowledged Teacher of the authentic principles for happiness.

First of all, he said that those who are poor spiritually are happier, for to them belongs the Kingdom of Heaven. That is to say, those who have a feeling of spiritual need are open to receive all the spiritual riches of Christ's kingdom. He will pour blessings upon those who have such a real and humble sense of need.

Secondly, the Beatitudes tell us that those who mourn shall be happy. It seems rather strange to say that a person who is sad because of mourning can be happy. But the wonderful fact is that such a bereaved and sad person will be comforted by the great and loving God, and in a way that goes beyond all human consolation. As a result his tears will be dried and his sorrow will presently be turned into gladness. The really deep meaning here is that only those who have suffered sorrow and mourning can experience that depth of comfort which produces exquisite happiness. The counterpart of sorrow is joy, and it is in the blending of these intense experiences that life acquires its richest meaning. Only Jesus could have thought of this and expressed it so well.

The word *comfort* also implies strengthening as well as consolation. Those who bear sorrow patiently grow in patience, and if you sorrow for others you develop compassion. And the love that results causes you to feel deeply happy in the heart.

A third beatitude or blessed truth spoken by Jesus is that the meek are happy, for the Lord loves meekness and they will receive so bountifully from God that it is almost like inheriting the earth.

Of course, those people who heard Jesus say this must have been astonished, for they had always believed that the only way to get what you wanted was by force, power, and by being aggressive. But Jesus came up with the brand-new principle that meekness and humility and self-sacrifice will get you further, for then people will love and trust you. Meekness at last proves irresistible and leads to wider influence than the crude method of aggressively trying to lord it over people.

The fourth beatitude promises happiness to those who deeply hunger for a righteous life, who want goodness as they want water when thirsty. Those whose chief desire is to do what God wishes will become very happy, for God will fully satisfy their deepest desires. There will be no unfulfilled longings; their lives will be filled to overflowing with blessings.

Another way to happiness is outlined in the fifth beatitude, and that is to show mercy to other people. Don't try to get even with them, Jesus told his hearers; don't make it hard for them. Refrain from any kind of cruel attitude or treatment. Be nice to people. Be kindly, thoughtful, loving, and considerate. As a result people will tend to treat you in a similar fashion. But more important still, God will be merciful to you even when you fail to deserve such consideration. He will be kind and will show His love to you by not treating you other than in a merciful manner.

A further great truth spoken by Jesus in the Sermon on the Mount is of vast importance because it involves our closeness to God. Since we are children of God, the unhappiest person is the one who is farthest from God, the one who is most alienated. Between God and him is a magnified generation gap; he is far from a happy feeling of unity with his Heavenly Father. The way to put right this sad state of affairs is to purify the heart of every element that is at odds with God's pure nature. Then, when the heart is purified, one will be able to "see" God or to have full insight into God's mind and heart, and as a result feel very close to Him. There is no happiness in the world that equals a close, deep, and unbroken relationship with God, who gives life and watches over each one always.

Still another happy group are those who help bring peace to the world. They are the reconcilers among men whose goal it is to persuade everyone to live with all people in brotherly goodwill and understanding. Today the peacemakers include those who strive to heal divisions among the races and who work in all nations to find alternatives to war. They show how people can get along better through mutual respect and peaceful discussion rather than by hostility and force. Such people, God says, are His sons. They really please Him and so by their peace-making they become deeply happy inwardly.

Finally, this happy life promised by Jesus includes being willing to be persecuted because of your convictions. If you stand up for your principles and have what it takes to endure opposition and hostility and never waver, you will have all the riches Heaven can bestow.

Indeed, you will enjoy an inward un-alloyed happiness even when people insult and mistreat you, even when they lie about you and make it rough for you. Stick it out. Be true to Christ and his principles and you will be rewarded here on earth and in Heaven. You will be a truly happy person.

Subtle principles such as the Beatitudes mark Jesus Christ as the most astute teacher of all time. And those who live by these principles win out in that greatest of all human adventures, the quest for happiness.

In a way, the Sermon on the Mount is an elaboration of the two great principles that Jesus referred to constantly during his life on earth. One of those principles is love. The other is faith.

To love God, Jesus said, and to love your neighbor as yourself, these are the two basic commandments. It is easy to see why. Love neutralizes fear, anger, hostility, resentment—all the negative emotions that cripple and handicap people. Love would wipe out war, if we would just let it. It will conquer any enemy, including the greatest enemy

that most of us have to face: ourselves. Love was the reason Christ came into the world. Love was the reason he died on the cross. God, he taught us, is love. That was the gospel, the "good news" that he came to preach.

The other great principle that Jesus tried to get across to us is the power of belief. To this day, most of us haven't fully grasped the meaning of what he said, although he said it plainly enough, over and over. Here is how he put it in the twenty-third verse of the ninth chapter of Mark's gospel: "If thou canst believe, all things are possible to him that believeth."

Study this verse well, because in it we are offered something tremendous. Jesus didn't say *some* things, he said *all* things. In another amazing statement, he said that if anyone had enough faith, he could tell a mountain to throw itself into the sea, and the mountain would obey. Some people think he was speaking figuratively, but I believe that he meant what he said, literally, concretely, exactly.

It's an extraordinary promise, but there's a condition, an "if" in it. *If* you can believe, then all things are possible. This implies that true believing, complete believing, is very difficult. Not even the apostles could always do it. When they failed to heal people or cast out demons, and asked Jesus why, he told them that their faith wasn't strong enough.

So deep faith requires tremendous mental discipline. It requires giving your whole self to it. It isn't something you can achieve with just the surface of your mind. It doesn't come from the glib recital of a creed.

But I am absolutely convinced, and have preached all my life, that if you can overcome your doubt, your negativisms, your fears, and replace them with deep belief, you will thereby enter into a life transformed.

Jesus himself said, "He that believeth on me, the works that I do shall he do also: and greater works than these shall he do.

What a promise, if we can only claim it— by the magic of belief!

The Storm Clouds Gather

The weeks and months went by. Jesus moved from place to place, teaching, healing, sending out his disciples to do the same. He had no permanent home; he once said that the birds of the air had their nests, and the foxes their holes, but he had no place to lay his head. Larger and larger grew the crowds that followed him. Now and then, alone or with one or two of his disciples, he would withdraw to some lonely place to rest and pray.

On one such occasion, alone with Peter and James and John on a high mountain, the Bible says that he was transfigured before them, "and his face did shine as the sun, and his raiment was white as the light." The dazzled disciples saw two figures talking with Jesus whom they recognized as Moses and Elijah, and they were terrified. But Jesus came and touched them, and told them not to be afraid. "And when they had lifted up their eyes, they saw no man, save Jesus only."

It must have been hard for the disciples to reconcile such stupendous happenings with the human side of Jesus, their daily companion and beloved leader and friend. They saw him transfigured on the mountain, talking to mighty prophets long dead. But they also saw him at dinner with ordinary people, letting children climb into his lap, establishing warm and loving relationships with men everywhere.

Women were his close friends too. In ancient times women were almost universally considered inferior to men, but Jesus always treated them with great gentleness. Even when their conduct was questionable or their reputation stained, he was compassionate.

Once, hoping that this compassion would bring Jesus into conflict with Mosaic law, the Pharisees brought to him a woman accused of being unfaithful to her husband. The penalty for adultery was death. "This woman is guilty," the Pharisees said to Jesus. "There is no doubt about it. The Law of Moses says she should be stoned to death. What do you say?"

Jesus looked at the trembling woman, full of fear and shame. Then he looked at the Pharisees. Knowing what was in their hearts, he did not answer them at all. Instead, he stooped down and began to write in the dust with his finger. What did he write? The Bible doesn't say. It has been suggested that perhaps he wrote a list of secret sins that each of the Pharisees had committed. Whatever it was, the impression on the woman's accusers was profound. As they stood there in silence, Jesus looked up and said, "Let the one among you who has never sinned cast the first stone at her." Then he went on writing on the ground.

Gradually, one by one, the Pharisees slunk away until only the woman was left. "Well," said Jesus to her, "where are your accusers? Does no one condemn you?"

There was a flicker of hope in the terrified woman's eyes as she replied, "No one, sir."

"I don't condemn you either," Jesus said gently. "Go on home—and do not sin again."

On another occasion, when Jesus was having dinner in the house of a Pharisee named Simon, a woman of the town with a very bad reputation heard he was there. Somehow she gained admittance and stood behind him, crying. She had brought with her an alabaster flask of expensive perfume with which to anoint Jesus' feet. Still weeping, she knelt before him, and as her tears fell on his feet she wiped them away with her hair.

Simon, the host, said to himself, "If my guest of honor were really a prophet, he would know what a bad woman this really is."

Jesus knew what he was thinking. "Simon," he said, "let me tell you a story. Once upon a time there were two men, both in debt to a moneylender. One owed him ten times as much as the other. Since neither could pay, the kindhearted money-lender canceled both debts. Which man do you think was the most grateful?"

"I suppose," said Simon, "the one who owed the most."

"You are right" Jesus said. He went on to point out that, sinful though she was, the woman had offered him all the love she had. Those who love much, he told Simon, are forgiven much. Then he said to the woman, "Your faith has saved you. Go in peace."

The more the crowds flocked to Jesus, and the more his fame and popularity grew, the more the religious leaders resented him.

In the first place, they were jealous. Their own sterile expressions of religion could not compete with the warmth of the message of love and faith that Jesus preached so eloquently. Their own obsession with rules and rituals had created an emotional vacuum in the people's hearts. When Jesus filled it, they were enraged.

In the second place, whenever they tried to entrap Jesus, he made them look foolish— and nothing infuriates pompous men more. Time and again they tried to make him say things that would alienate the people from him. Once they asked him craftily if it was lawful for the Jews to pay tribute to the Roman emperor. They thought that if he said yes, the common people would be angry. If he said no, they hoped the Romans would arrest him for treason. Calmly Jesus asked for a coin (clearly he carried no money of his own). When a Roman penny was handed to him, he pointed to the profile of the emperor stamped upon it. "Give what is Caesar's to Caesar," he said. "And to God, what is God's." His enemies were speechless.

On another occasion, when they asked him by what authority he taught (the chief priests were obsessed with the idea that all moral teaching had to be based on Scripture as they interpreted it), Jesus answered their question with a question. Speaking of his dead cousin, John the Baptist, he said, "Tell me, was John's baptism from Heaven or from men?" In other words, was he just an ordinary man, or was he really a prophet speaking God's truth through inspiration? The Pharisees stared at one another. If they admitted that John was a true prophet, Jesus would then ask, "Why don't you believe what he said about me?" If they said he was a mere man, the people would be infuriated because they believed that John had indeed been a prophet. They muttered feebly that they couldn't answer Jesus' question. "Well, then," said Jesus with his quiet smile, "why should I answer yours?"

One of the Pharisees' chief complaints about Jesus was that he did not let rigid rules about the Sabbath keep him from healing or helping people on that day. Over and over again this conflict arose.

On one Sabbath day, Jesus met a man who had been blind from birth. Feeling sorry for him, the Master Healer made a kind of clay out of dust and his own spittle, put it on the blind man's eyes, and told him to go and wash in a pool called Siloam, which means "one who has been sent." When the man obeyed, his sight was restored. The Pharisees claimed angrily that Jesus could not be from God since he did not observe the Sabbath. But the man who had been healed spoke up forcibly. "God doesn't listen to sinners," he said. "He listens only to those who do what He wants them to do. Since the beginning of time, no one born blind has ever received his sight. But this has happened to me. If this man Jesus doesn't come from God, he couldn't do such things!"

The unanswerable logic of this enraged the Pharisees all the more, and they expelled the former blind man from the synagogue.

On another occasion when Jesus was preaching in the synagogue on the Sabbath there was a man in the congregation who had a withered hand. The Pharisees were watching closely to see if Jesus would heal him (perhaps they had even "planted" him there), and Jesus knew this. He called the

man to the front of the congregation. Then he turned to the Pharisees. "Does the Law command us to do good on the Sabbath," he asked, "or to do harm? Does it require us to save life or destroy it?" Nobody answered. He looked slowly around with those marvelous penetrating eyes, but still nobody spoke. Then he said to the man, "Stretch out your hand!" The man did so, and in that instant the withered hand was completely restored.

Such episodes fanned the anger of the religious leaders to a white-hot fury. There may have been some of these men who honestly feared that Jesus' ministry might come to be regarded by the Romans as the beginning of some kind of rebellion against Rome, and that it might lead to repression that would cause the Jews to lose what little liberty they still had. But most of the antagonism was based on fear of change, resentment of anything new, and jealousy of Jesus as a supremely successful preacher and teacher. The religious hierarchy decided that, one way or another, they would have to get rid of him.

Clearly, this would not be easy to do. For one thing, the people might easily rise up to defend him and turn on them. Besides, preaching the love of God was no crime. Healing the sick was no crime. Raising people from the dead was no crime. Even if they caused Jesus to be arrested on some such charge as breaking the rules concerning the Sabbath, that would not silence him or put an end to his ministry. Even if they accused him of blasphemy, the Jews no longer had the right to inflict capital punishment on anyone. The Romans reserved that grim privilege for themselves.

But perhaps, the high priests told one another, if they arrested Jesus secretly, they might be able to find some way to persuade the Romans to execute him. So, like patient spiders weaving an evil web, they bided their time.

Knowing all this, Jesus was well aware that the city of Jerusalem, where the priests were most powerful, had become a death trap for him. And the mortal man in him

shrank from exposing himself to the fate that he knew awaited him. But the divine person also knew what his death would have meant for mankind, and his obedience to the will of his Heavenly Father never wavered.

The feast of the Passover was approaching; Jerusalem was crowded with visitors and pilgrims. The raising of Lazarus from the dead was still a burning topic of conversation. Some swore that it had really happened. Others insisted that it was impossible. Everyone wanted to see the extraordinary person now known as the Prophet of Nazareth.

When the common people heard that Jesus was coming to Jerusalem for the Passover despite the order that had been put out for his arrest, they were overjoyed. Some hoped that he would use his supernatural powers to overwhelm his priestly enemies. Others were convinced that he would use the occasion of the Passover to throw off the iron grip of Rome. The Messiah, they told one another excitedly, was to be a mighty king and liberator who would restore liberty and justice and reign forever. Perhaps this glorious day was at hand. Perhaps they would see these mighty events with their own eyes. No wonder they lined the roads. No wonder they tore down palm branches and threw them down to make a verdant path as Jesus came riding by. No wonder they shouted themselves hoarse, hailing him as the son of David, and their King.

But already Judas, one of the chosen twelve disciples, had gone to the high priests and for a reward of thirty pieces of silver had agreed to deliver Jesus into their hands, or at least to point him out to them at a time when it would be safe to arrest him. Thirty pieces of silver—the price of one man's life. In those days, if a man killed another man's slave, he had to pay thirty pieces of silver to the slave's owner. Perhaps this was the reason that amount was agreed upon.

Why did Judas betray his Lord and Master? Was he simply greedy for money? In his Gospel Saint John says that Judas was in charge of the small amounts of money that the disciples had, and that he was not above stealing from it. Was it a matter of thwarted ambition—was he angry because Jesus refused to make himself into a king and his disciples into powerful princes? Did he believe that the betrayal might force Jesus to use his mighty powers to defend himself and so gain universal recognition as the Messiah? Or, as the Bible says, did Satan simply take possession of this man, creeping in through some fatal flaw in his character? Whatever his reasons, whatever his motives, the name of Judas has lived and will live in infamy for all time.

Day after day during the week before Passover, Jesus appeared openly in the temple, and the high priests were afraid to make a move. It was on one of these visits that he became angry with the moneychangers and sellers of sacrificial animals who had taken over parts of the sacred building, chattering, bargaining, fleecing unsuspecting pilgrims and worshipers whenever they could. He overturned the tables of the moneychangers. The coins must have gone bouncing and ringing about the floor, but no one dared to stand up to this man whose eyes flashed with indignation and whose powerful arms rippled with the muscles hardened by years of toil in the carpenter's shop. Not a voice was raised in answer as he thundered, "It is written, My house shall be called the house of prayer; but ye have made it a den of thieves!" I have always thought that artists who have depicted Jesus as weak or frail-looking must have overlooked this passage altogether.

But time was running out, and Jesus knew it. He had warned his disciples that he would be arrested, tried, and executed, but they could not bring themselves to believe it. Nor did they understand when he said that on the third day after his apparent death he would rise again.

Confused but loyal, they waited to see what would happen next. They did not have to wait long.

The Darkest Night

Let's say that you are a follower of Jesus Christ in the year A.D. 28 or 29. You have a house in Jerusalem where occasionally you rent out a large upper room for gatherings of one kind or another. Word has come to you that the Master wishes to use this room to celebrate the Passover with his closest associates.

You are thriiled and honored, you have made everything ready, the room is spotlessly clean, the food is prepared. But you are also worried. Rumors are flying around the city. Some people say that the high priests have decided to ignore Jesus, that he is so popular with the people that they are afraid to take action against him. Others insist that they are just waiting for an opportunity to pounce. Still others whisper that Roman spies are watching everything since the disturbance in the temple when Jesus drove out the moneychangers. If those spies are really shadowing Jesus, if they know where he intends to observe the Passover, may they also not be watching your house? May there not be a sudden, dreadful knock on your door in the middle of the feast? Who knows?

These are tense and dangerous times.

But you are willing to risk your life, even your family's lives, because you have heard this man preach, you have seen the astounding miracles he has performed, you have felt the love and warmth that surround him, and you are convinced that he is indeed the Messiah, the Son of God. So as the thirteen figures come into your house out of the purple twilight, you welcome them as they come in, led by the Master himself: Peter and his brother, Andrew, their rugged faces weatherbeaten from years spent in open boats; then James and John, the highstrung, impetuous sons of Zebedee; then Thomas with his wary, questioning look; then Matthew the former tax collector; then Philip and Bartholomew; James, the son of Alpheus; Simon, called the patriot; Judas, the son of James; and finally, last of all, Jadas Iscariot, with his dark, brooding face. You show them into the upper room. Then you retire to the kitchen to make sure that all is in order.

This last meal that Jesus shared with his disciples is one of the great events in

Christian history. Ever since, Christians all over the world have gathered to commemorate this Passover meal shared so long ago by Christ and his twelve disciples, that commemoration being known variously as Holy Communion, the Holy Eucharist, and the Lord's Supper.

Of the accounts in the four gospels, Saint John's is the longest and the most vivid. He tells how Jesus astonished his followers by kneeling down in a gesture of love and humility and washing their feet. They had been arguing among themselves as to who was the greatest, and this simple act was designed to show them that the greatest was also the one who served others most.

Next he told them, quietly and resignedly that one of them was going to betray him. Eleven of the men who heard him could not believe their ears; they kept asking, in shock and distress, "Lord, is it I?" But one man knew very well what Jesus meant. When Jesus looked straight at Judas and said, "Do what you intend to do quickly," the traitor left the room and headed straight for the palace of Caiaphas, the high priest.

With the poisonous presence of Judas removed, an atmosphere of deep love and fellowship filled the upper room. Quietly, tenderly, Jesus spoke to these honest, troubled men who had followed him so long and so trustingly. In a few simple words, he summed up the whole of his message to them—and to all of us: "A new commandment I give unto you, that ye love one another; as I have loved you...."

He told them that shortly he would be leaving them, that they could not follow him now (although they could later), that he would prepare a place for them where they could all be together.

"Lord," cried the impetuous Peter, "why cannot I follow thee now?" He knew that Jesus was speaking of his own death. "I will lay down my life," he added passionately, "for thy sake."

Jesus looked at Peter with love and pity. He told him gently that before the cock crowed the next morning, Peter would have denied his Lord and Master three times.

Another disciple, Thomas, shook his head slowly. He didn't understand where Jesus was going, or how the rest of them could get there. Again Jesus answered with words that lie at the heart of the Christian reliogion: "I am the way, the truth, and the life: no man cometh unto the Father, but by me."

Bread and wine were on the table. Here are Saint Luke's words describing the beginning of a ceremony that has no end: "And he took bread, and gave thanks, and brake it, and gave unto them, saying, This is my body which is given for you: this do in remembrance of me. Likewise also the cup after supper, saying, This cup is the new testament in my blood, which is shed for you."

When the meal was over, they sang a hymn. Then they went out into the chilly night. Across the brook Kidron, on the Mount of Olives, was a garden called Gethsemane—in Aramaic the word means "oil press." Jesus and his disciples often used it as a meeting place, and Judas the betrayer was well aware of this.

Near the entrance to the garden, Jesus left eight of the disciples behind. With Peter, James and John he moved on through the shadows. It must have been dark under the trees, with only faint glints of moonlight or starshine coming through. He halted finally, asking his three closest friends to wait and watch. Then he moved forward a little distance and fell on the ground and prayed.

Foreknowledge would be a terrible thing for any man. In Jesus such knowledge was complete, and the events that he foresaw were so dreadful that the mortal man in him was appalled. Desperately he prayed that, even at this late hour, he might somehow be spared such a frightful ordeal. But he also prayed that the will of his Father might prevail—and this was the prayer that was answered.

No one knows exactly how long this mental anguish continued. Saint Luke, the physician, tells us that "his sweat was as it were great drops of blood falling down to the ground." When at last he arose, calm and in full possession of himself, he found that the three disciples, worn out by tension and anxiety, had fallen asleep.

By now it was too late to make any difference. Torches flared in the dark. There was a jangling of armor and weapons and the thud of heavy footsteps as the temple guard

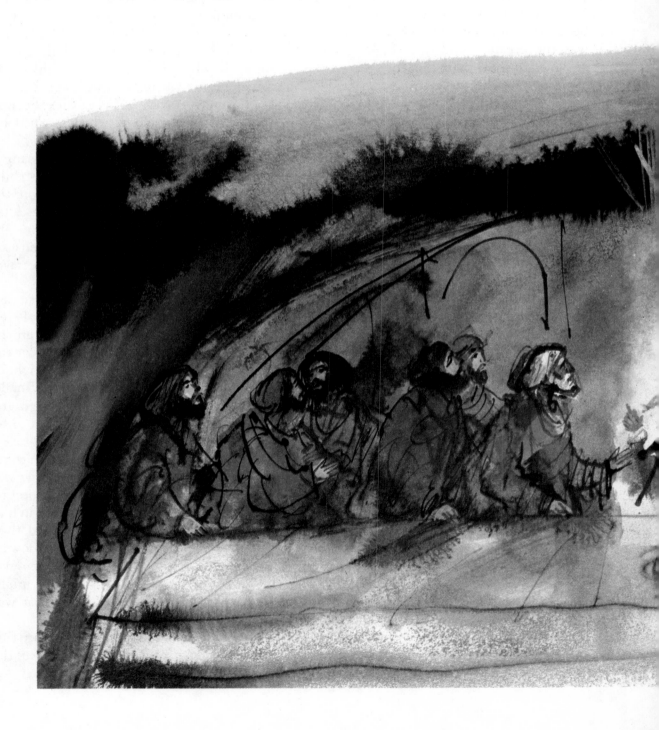

came crashing through the olive trees with Judas leading them. The commanding figure of Jesus was easily recognizable in the sudden light. Judas went straight up to him and kissed him, a form of betrayal so repulsive that even Jesus found it hard to believe that such vileness could exist. "Judas," he said bitterly, "do you really betray the Son of Man with a kiss?"

There was a momentary flurry of resistance among the panic-stricken disciples. Peter drew a sword and struck at one of the

servants of the high priest, cutting off his ear. But Jesus ordered them not to use violence, and they fled into the protective shadows.

His hands bound with cords, Jesus was led away to the house of the high priest. No angry crowds gathered to demand his release; it was too late at night. Peter had fled with the other disciples, but now he summoned up enough courage to follow the receding torches— at a distance. One other disciple, probably John, was known to the household of the high priest and admitted to the courtyard. He persuaded the maid at the door to admit Peter. She looked suspiciously at the big fisherman. "Aren't you a follower of that man?" she demanded. "Not I," mumbled Peter, shouldering his way past her.

While Jesus was being questioned and falsely accused inside the building, Peter joined a group at a fire that had been built in the courtyard to ward off the chill of the night air. As he stood there warming himself and trying to look inconspicuous, a member of the group accused him of being a friend of Jesus. Again Peter denied it. An hour later, the same thing happened. This time Peter cursed and swore, ranting that he had never even met Jesus.

As he made this third denial, a door opened and Jesus, still bound and surrounded by guards, was led through the courtyard. Just at that moment, in the sudden hush when all eyes were on the prisoner, thin and lonely in the cold air came the sound of a

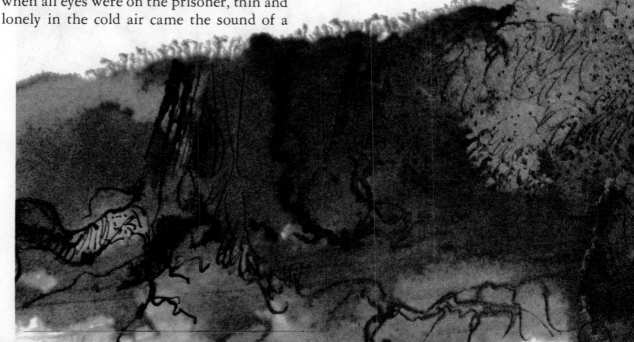

distant cock crowing. And, says the Bible, "the Lord turned, and looked upon Peter."

There was no accusation, no condemnation in that gaze, only pity and compassion, but Peter was struck to the heart. Trying to hold back his tears, muffling his face in his cloak, he stumbled to the door and out into the silent night. The hour before dawn, they say, is the darkest of all. But the darkness of that hour was as nothing compared to the darkness and desolation in the soul of this warm-hearted man who knew that he had permitted fear to triumph over love.

He "remembered the word of the Lord, how he had said to him, Before the cock crow, thou shalt deny me thrice. And Peter went out, and wept bitterly."

"Crucify Him!"

By the time the sun rose on the day before the Sabbath, the religious leaders in Jerusalem had condemned their prisoner to death. Such a sentence could not be carried out except by order of the Roman governor. So while it was still very early, they brought Jesus to Pontius Pilate.

During the long night, Jesus had been mocked, reviled, buffeted, and spat upon. The servants of the high priest had blindfolded him and slapped him, crying, "You're supposed to be a great prophet. Prophesy who struck you!" So the pinioned man who was led through the streets in the early sunlight was weary, bruised, and beaten. Even so, he held his head high, and there was a quiet dignity about him that even the rough soldiers who hurried him along found impressive.

Pilate found it impressive too. Although he was there to govern them, he had an arrogant Roman's distaste for the emperor's subjects. To him they seemed obsessed with their religion, always arguing or fighting or complaining about various aspects of it. They were emotionally volatile, too, and restive under the Roman yoke. Among such people, Pilate thought as he stared at the bruised face and torn garments of Jesus, one madman could incite a full-scale rebellion. He went out of the hall of judgment and faced the muttering crowd outside. "What accusation do you bring against this man?" he demanded.

The high priests gave an answer that showed Pilate instantly the weakness of their case. "If he weren't a criminal," they shouted, "we wouldn't have brought him here!"

"Why bother me with him?" asked Pilate angrily. "You have your own law. Take him and judge him according to it."

"We can't put any man to death," was the answer. "And he deserves to die. He told the people that they shouldn't pay tribute to Caesar. He calls himself a king."

Pilate hesitated. Self-appointed kings could be dangerous. Back he went and talked to Jesus again, trying to find out who this strange man was and what his aims and purposes were. Jesus told him quietly that he had come into the world to bear witness to the truth. Pilate gave a world-weary shrug. "What is truth?" he asked cynically.

If he had waited a few moments, he might have had an answer that would have changed his life. But he wanted to get this unpleasant affair over with. He went back to the accusers and told them that he could find no fault in Jesus.

Frantic lest their victim escape, they howled that Jesus had stirred up trouble all the way from Galilee to Jerusalem. When he learned that Jesus was a Galilean, Pilate thought he saw a chance to pass the buck. He sent the prisoner to Herod, the tetrarch of Galilee, who happened to be in Jerusalem. Herod was fascinated to see Jesus, because he had heard so much about him. But when Jesus refused to answer his questions, or to

perform miracles on demand, Herod sent him back to Pilate.

Pilate was exasperated to find the problem back on his hands. As a compromise measure, he decided to have Jesus scourged in order to satisfy the bloodlust of the mob. Then he intended to let him go.

Scourging with the brutal, metal-tipped lash that the Romans used was almost worse that capital punishment. It slashed a man's back to ribbons, cutting to the bone. In the cathedral of Turin, Italy, there is today a very ancient linen cloth that for centuries has been venerated as the burial shroud of Jesus. Originally it was impregnated with spices, as was the custom among the Jews in Jesus' time. Moisture on the body of a man who evidently died in great agony, with profuse sweating, apparently formed a chemical reaction that left a vivid impression on the linen, in effect a primitive photographic negative. The man was a victim of crucifixion, the spikes being driven not through the palms of the hands but through the wrists. Before his crucifixion he was cruelly whipped; the marks of the lash studded with numerous dumbbell-shaped bits of metal are gruesomely plain. The man's agony and loss of blood must have been fearful. The Bible does not go into such details. It simply says that Pilate had Jesus scourged.

The jeering soldiers took the fainting man, made a crown of thorns, put it on his head, dressed him in a purple robe, and pretended to bow down before him as if he were a king. Finally Pilate had him brought out to the waiting crowd. "Behold the man!" he said to them, in a remark full of

admiration.

What was his motive for this? Did he hope that when the mob saw how brutally Jesus had been beaten they would feel a pang of pity and agree to Pilate's proposal that he be released? Did the courage and dignity in the silent figure so impress the callous Roman that he thought these qualities might impress the accusers also? We can never know. All we know is that the mob refused Pilate's offer, demanding instead the release of a notorious bandit and murderer named Barabbas. "Crucify him!" they kept shrieking. "Crucify him!"

Pilate was not afraid of an unarmed mob; his soldiers could have dispersed them easily. What, then, made him give in? Was it the argument that unless he condemned Jesus he would be in the position of defending an enemy of Caesar? Was it the fact that his wife had had a disturbing dream about Jesus (this shows that his name must have been on every tongue in Jerusalem) and Pilate thought that Jesus might be capable of casting a spell on her? Or was it simply the governor's cynical feeling that the easiest way to be rid of the matters was to eliminate the cause, however innocent the cause might be?

He caused a basin of water to be brought and washed his hands in it. "Let this act bear witness to the fact that I am innocent of the blood of this man," he said. Then, without another qualm, he handed the innocent man over to be crucified.

The place of execution, a hill outside the city walls, bore the sinister name of Golgotha—"place of the skull." Exactly where it was is still a matter of debate, but wherever it was, the road that led to it was a pilgrimage of pain. The Romans had the grim practice of making a crucifixion victim carry his own cross. Some historians think that it was only the crossbar that was carried, the upright being already at the execution site. In any case the load was great—too great for a man who had already suffered what Jesus had suffered. After he had fallen several times, the soldiers collared a passer-by, one Simon of Cyrene, and made him carry the cross.

It was about noon when the bloodstained figure of Jesus was stretched out along the rough wood. His executioners had offered him a drink of wine mingled with myrrh, a kind of primitive painkiller, but he refused it. With an awful pounding the hammers drove the great spikes home, in terrible counterpoint to the sobbing of the women who had followed Jesus to the end. Two thieves, common criminals, were crucified at the same time, one on either side of him. The three crosses were raised to an upright position, the base of each one sliding with a cruel thud into the prepared hole in the ground. To those in the watching crowd who had hoped to the end that some miracle might yet occur, it must have seemed like the final collapse of all their hopes and dreams.

For the next three hours, in agony that we cannot even begin to imagine, Jesus hung on the cross. He spoke very seldom: only seven statements are attributed to him. Some of these were quotations from the Psalms that he loved. Others were expressions of sympathy and kindness for other people: he promised the crucified thief who appealed to him that they would be together after death; he instructed a grieving disciple to take care of his heartbroken mother. He even uttered words of sympathy for his persecutors: "Father, forgive them; for they know not what they do."

At this terrible moment in history, the forces of nature seemed to be grieving also. Darkness spread over the face of the land. Somewhere, in the awful silence, a limp form was swinging at the end of a rope: Judas, the traitor, overwhelmed by the horror of what he had done, had hanged himself. The Roman soldiers at the foot of the cross stared uneasily into the lowering sky. From Jesus' parched lips came a pathetic whisper: "I thirst." One of the soldiers dipped a sponge in sour wine, put it on the end of a reed, and held it up to his lips. Perhaps from it came a tiny flicker of relief, but it was too late. the head crowned with thorns fell forward. "It is finished," Jesus murmured, and his spirit left his tormented body.

At that very moment, the Scripture tells us, a violent earthquake rocked the land, so violent that even the graves in cemeteries were flung open. The centurion in charge of the executions stared in awe at the lifeless form on the cross. "Surely," he said, "that was truly the Son of God."

By now it was midafternoon, and at sundown the Sabbath began. To hasten the death of the crucified men, the soldiers broke the legs of the two thieves—hanging helplessly, they would suffocate—but when they came to Jesus he was dead already. To make sure, one soldier thrust a spear into his side, and the disciple John, who was standing there, tells us that "forthwith came there out blood and water."

Soon after that a disciple of Jesus named Joseph of Arimathea went to Pilate and asked permission to take the body of Jesus down from the cross and bury it. The Roman governor, perhaps frightened by the earthquake, perhaps burdened by a guilty conscience, made no objection.